# *Easy* HOME IMPROVEMENTS

# DIETER MYLIUS

# CONTENTS

EDITORIAL
Project Manager: Sandra Hartley
Editorial Co-ordinator:
Margaret Kelly
Project Editor: Sheridan Carter
Craft Editor: Tonia Todman
UK Editor: Martin Preston

DESIGN AND PRODUCTION
Nadia Sbisa
Monica Kessler-Tay
Chris Hatcher

PHOTOGRAPHY
Andrew Elton
(except where otherwise
credited)

ILLUSTRATIONS
Greg Gaul
Dieter Mylius

COVER
Frank Pithers (Design)
Andrew Elton (Photography)

PUBLISHER
Philippa Sandall

Published by J.B.Fairfax
Press Pty Ltd
80-82 McLachlan Avenue
Rushcutters Bay 2011

EASY HOME
IMPROVEMENTS
Includes Index
ISBN 1 86343 008 3

Formatted by J.B.Fairfax Press
Pty Ltd
Output by Adtype, Sydney
Printed by Toppan Printing Co,
Hong Kong
Distributed by J.B.Fairfax Press Ltd
9 Trinity Centre, Park Farm Estate
Wellingborough Northants
Ph: (0933) 402330
Fax: (0933) 402234

# INTRODUCTION

*R*oll on the weekend! A time to stop, put the feet up, enjoy a cool drink, close your eyes and ... sink into a deep sleep? Certainly not! It's time to dream up your next home improvement project .

Why working weekends? It's the natural time to undertake projects. Most of us only have the weekends to do work around the home. With this in mind, it is useful to know approximately how much time a project is going to take.

All of our projects outline at the beginning what you need to buy, the special tools needed and the approximate time involved. Each project has easy to follow step by step instructions, including pictures and diagrams and loads of special tips.

The projects in this book delve into a wide range of areas: including bricklaying, cabinetmaking, carpentry and joinery, finishing, interior design and decoration, interior lining, leadlighting, paving, tiling with various materials, and window and skylight installation.

Some projects are easy, some are more ambitious. Many can be undertaken using the simplest of tools. Lots of illustrations of other projects are presented simply as ideas to inspire.

Experienced do-it-yourselfers will be keen to undertake projects which involve a degree of difficulty, while beginners will want to start with something simple. The important thing is to have a go.

Fairly major projects, such as timber decks, and window and wall installation may require the go-ahead from your local council. You may be asked to submit plans for approval, apply for a building permit and pay fees. You must comply with any safety regulations or special legal requirements. Don't forget to stay in your neighbours' good books by keeping them informed, especially if your project will infringe on or disturb their privacy in some way.

Remember the golden rule: Measure once, measure twice!
Good preparation is everything.

*Before tackling any kind of home improvement, you will need to check your resources in terms of equipment. Do you have the right stuff? Following is a list of what should be found in a basic kit. Over time, your tool kit can be added to with every project – that way all your tools will be used.*

# THE RIGHT STUFF

## Setting up your tool kit

**Once your tools are in good order, keep them that way. See pages 6-7 on the care and safe handling of tools.**

If you are going to embark on a series of projects, the tools you purchase should be of medium quality at least. If you intend doing some very demanding work, buy only the best.

If you already have an extensive collection of tools, make sure they are sharp and ready for use. Old tools can be just as good but may need to be renovated and resharpened.

### WHAT TO BUY

■ **Hammer:** The hammer should be a claw hammer of light-to-medium weight. This type of hammer is used for driving in nails and stubborn objects. It may have a wooden, fibreglass or steel shaft. Before use, slightly roughen the head of the hammer with some emery cloth to ensure it does not skid off the nails. The claw of the hammer is used for extracting nails.

■ **Screwdrivers:** There are many available, but initially three will suffice. Two normal slot-type screwdrivers of 150 mm and 100 mm will undo most screws. Add to this a cross-head-type screwdriver, such as a Posidriv or Supadriv. If you have to drive or remove many screws, it may be worthwhile investing in a ratchet screwdriver. Electric screwdrivers are also available.

■ **Tape or rule:** Most people prefer to use retractable metal tapes, which are available with markings in both metric and imperial units. For some small jobs it may be easier to use a four-fold box rule, which folds out to a length of 1 m.

■ **Square:** Either a try or combination square for marking 90° and 45° angles.

■ **Level:** A level of between 450 mm and 900 mm for project work and installation of built-ins.

■ **Clamps:** Clamps may be 'G' clamps in a range of sizes from 100 mm to 250 mm, or adjustable sliding clamps. Sash clamps are only limited by the length of the bar (which may be water pipe).

■ **Vice:** Two types of vice are available. The woodworking vice is permanently bolted to the workbench and sits flush with the benchtop. The jaws of the vice are often 'softened' with either plastic or timber blocks. The other type of vice is an engineer's vice – this is bolted to the top of the workbench. This type is designed for metalwork but with jaw liners can be adapted for minor woodwork.

■ **Panel saw:** This is the most useful wood- or wood-panel cutting saw, usually around 450 mm long, with approximately ten teeth to 25 mm, referred to as 'ten-point'. Similar in appearance to the panel saw is the cross-cut saw, which is sharpened specifically to cut across the grain of timber. Other saws, such as the fine tenon saw for joinery, the hacksaw for cutting metal, the power circular saw for volume cutting and the jig saw for curved cutting, can be bought if needed.

■ **Utility knife:** For

cutting; featuring a fixed, interchangeable or 'snap-off' blade.

■ **Chisels:** Chisels should be of a reasonable quality as they will undergo rough treatment. There are special chisels for individual tasks. A good starting point is to obtain a 6 mm, 12 mm and 19 mm bevel-edged chisel. New chisels will generally need to be sharpened before use. Other sizes and shapes can be bought if it becomes necessary. A cold chisel is for chipping stone and concrete.

■ **Planes:** The most popular is the No. 4 smoothing plane with a cast metal body. This plane is about 200 mm long. A good plane is easy and accurate to use and holds its edge well. Special planes are available, but unless they are found in grandfather's old collection of tools, they are probably not worth acquiring. These include German jack planes, small hand-smoothing planes, and long steel trying planes. Most of the special rebating and routing planes have now been replaced by electric routers.

■ **Oil stone:** The combination medium-and-fine stone is best for keeping chisels and planes sharp. You will also need a small can of oil for oiling the stone. Oil stones should never be used dry. It is recommended that you use light machine oil. A mixture of oil and paraffin will also do the job.

■ **Drill:** Most useful would be a two-speed power drill with a chuck capacity of 10 mm or 13 mm. Hammer action, if you can afford it, is also helpful for drilling masonry. The slow speed should be 900 rpm or slower.

■ **Putty knife:** A range of different filling knives for applying fillers, plaster or synthetic wood.

■ **Brushes:** A small selection of brushes for dusting, touching up and broad-area painting.

■ **Pliers:** The first pair bought should have an insulated handle, and a length of 150 mm. General-purpose pliers will grip both flat and small round objects, and usually incorporate a wire cutter. There is a huge range of special-purpose pliers available – often for only one particular application – and these should be bought only when they are actually needed.

■ **Power tools:** The most useful, initially, are the bench grinder, electric drill, and the jig saw (see above). Others, such as a circular saw, router, power planer, electric screwdriver, laminate trimmer, angle grinder and power sanders can follow when necessary.

1 Panel saw, 2 Level, 3 Try square, 4 Plane, 5 Woodworking vice, 6 Clamps, 7 Pliers, 8 Adhesives (PVA, contact, 2 part epoxy), 9 Nails, 10 Screws, 11 Tape, 12 Brushes, 13 Chisels, 14 Putty knife, 15 Utility knife, 16 Oil stone and oil, 17 Abrasive papers, 18 Screwdrivers, 19 Bench grinder, 20 Jig saw, 21 Speed drill

# CARE AND SAFETY

*Having tools is great, but they do require a certain amount of care and common-sense treatment. The following pointers should help you look after your investment.*

There is nothing more frustrating than planning a project and getting everything ready, only to discover that the saw needs sharpening and the chisels have chunks missing out of them! Worse still, you've lent that essential tool to a friend who is on three weeks holiday!

Tools should be stored in a moisture-free place where little fingers that have no business touching them cannot reach. Do not let small children get their hands on your tools. A pegboard tool storage board and a tool carryall are both projects which feature in this book. They will help, although the ideal is to have a workroom. Most of us have to make do with a corner of the garage.

■ Keep all iron and steel surfaces lightly oiled. A wipe over every now and again with an oily rag will keep these surfaces in good condition. An alternative is to use moisture-excluding sprays or penetrating oils.

■ All wooden handles should be protected from splitting and drying out. The occasional coat of varnish or linseed oil to keep moisture in the timber will help.

■ Sharpened tools, such as chisels, are best kept in individual leather pouches to protect their edges, and your fingers. If you don't have pouches, let them hang by the handle in a position where the cutting edge will not contact anything else.

■ All screwdrivers, awls, pliers and similar tools can easily be kept in the carryall.

■ Saws should have their teeth protected from other tools. A good method is to use slide-on poster grips as these are self-supporting.

■ Planes should always be stored on their sides. Even if the blade is retracted, putting planes on their side is a good habit to get into, as invariably one day you will be too busy to retract the blade.

## GREEN TIPS

❧ Consider using recycled timber. Timber can be bought from demolition sites for a cheap price. As a bonus, often the timber bought at such a site is better than new lengths. Old timber from more mature trees has fewer knots. It is simple to work around notches, and denailing is not a difficult task.

❧ Exotic timber is a limited resource. We have a responsibility to make this limited resource go as far as possible. If the timber is being used for decorative purposes, much more will be available if it is sliced as a veneer and adhered to particleboard or medium-density fibreboard as a cheap backing. For instance, it is possible to provide twenty-five veneered table tops for every 25 mm solid table top. The chips to make particleboard can be taken from reject timber and thinnings.

❧ Think twice before using adhesives to hold things together. In many cases they must be used but, where they are not necessary, bear in mind that items will be easier to separate, and therefore to reuse, if mechanically held with screws or nails. When panelling is adhered to frames, the panelling will never be able to be reused. Do, however, consider laminating small pieces of timber together to form larger ones, e.g. wide boards, blocks and the like.

❧ Hardwoods are often selected because of their relative durability. However, CCA-treated pine will give equal, if not better, durability, and is a plantation species rather than a species from a dwindling, non-commercial forest.

❧ To save energy at home, consider insulation. Glass fibre, rockwool and cellulose are safe materials. Ceiling insulation will certainly help retain winter warmth and keep out summer heat. Wall insulation is less effective, but in climates with severe conditions is well worth considering.

❧ If you are in a position to build or extend, face the major glass areas towards where the sun will be at midday – north in the Southern Hemisphere and south in the Northern Hemisphere.

❧ When buying timber, find out from your local forestry department if a species suitable for your purpose is being culled.

❧ When buying goods from hardware stores, avoid those that are prepackaged in plastic and cardboard display packs, or those where you have to buy more than you need to. There are still stores around where they will sell you exactly the number of screws you want, and you can take the items away in your own bag or pocket.

## SAFETY

When doing any handy work make sure the work area is safe. It should be as level as possible, and you should not have to stretch for anything. Being off balance is dangerous when holding building materials and using tools. Make sure you have a first aid kit nearby.

Make sure that your clothing or hair cannot be caught up in the tools or work. Thongs or sandals should be barred from all do-it-yourself projects.

Many jobs involve sawdust or sharp chips which in certain instances can travel considerable distances when propelled by tools. For this reason, the operator should also wear appropriate face protection in the way of goggles and breathing masks when working with materials that may chip, splinter, create dangerous dust and odours, or splash or spray. In certain instances ear muffs and gloves are also recommended.

A general rule with most tools is to drive them away from you rather than towards you. That way if anything slips, it will be moving away from the body.

It is important that tools are sharp. More accidents occur using blunt tools than sharp ones, because blunt tools have to be forced to do the job. This is when they slip, and cause injury.

Always keep a close eye on children when working with tools.

## HOLDING YOUR WORK

Making projects at home is fine, but to work on timber and metal you will need somewhere to work and to hold materials down. Working on the floor can be backbreaking.

A workbench is ideal if you have the room. It should be sturdy, framed of large-section timbers, and be well braced to ensure it doesn't wobble. The top can be made, at least in part, of particleboard (chipboard) or plywood, but the front is best made of a more substantial pine or similar timber, about 200 mm x 75 mm. The timber should not be too hard, but solid enough to enable you to hammer and chop without marking the material you are working on. A wood vice can be fitted to the front edge on one end or, if you prefer, an engineer's vice can be

used instead.

A pair of saw-horses or stools will be most useful for many of the projects in this book. While making a pair of saw-stools is an interesting exercise, perhaps the first two should be bought – either ready-made up, or as a kit, so that you will quickly have a suitable surface for working on lengths of timber and panels.

We have already mentioned clamps, and they are well suited to use in conjunction with the stools.

Other jobs will require ladders or trestles, and these can be bought or hired when necessary. For jobs such as panelling the staircase, a combination ladder will be useful. When using extension ladders on finish work, pad the two top ends well with foam and old cloths to ensure they do not mark the work.

## CHECKLIST FOR POWER TOOLS

Power tools are a special case safety-wise because accidents tend to occur much more quickly and are often more serious.

❑ Make sure that all power points used are properly earthed, and that all wiring is in top order. If in doubt, have an electrician check the circuits.

❑ When using power tools, consider the use of a safety adaptor with RCD protection between the tool and the power outlet, so that if an accident occurs, the power will be interrupted in less than a heartbeat. You cannot always rely on fuses

to do the job – they protect property, not necessarily humans.

❑ Make sure the tool is in good condition. Do not use any power tool that has any exterior covers missing, or that has safety guards removed or inoperable. Do not overload the tool – if it loses speed, perhaps it can't cope with what is being demanded of it. Never stall a power tool.

❑ All adjustments and changing of bits and blades should be done with the tool disconnected from the power source.

❑ Beware of any tool grabbing or kicking back. This is always a possibility, for instance when drilling thin metal, or cutting along a length of timber with a circular saw. Never be in a position directly behind the saw, where the kick back can cause the saw to come into contact with you.

❑ Ensure that extension leads are unrolled entirely when in use, because if kept in a tight coil they can heat up considerably. Keep leads away from cutting blades. Be extra careful with extension leads and power tools being used near water such as pools or even wet grass.

❑ Always allow a tool to stop before putting it down. A coasting tool can grab, and perhaps come in contact with the operator or a bystander.

❑ Do not block off the ventilation holes or slots in a power tool, even when holding it, as it may overheat. Use the handles provided.

### Tool storage

*Tool storage is always a concern, especially when one contemplates the absolute mess that a workshop and workbench can quickly get into with nowhere to put things. A pegboard is simple to make and a low-cost storage solution for all your tools and other bits and pieces.*

*Project 1*

# Pegboard

**The project involves making a pegboard hanging board with a shelf and screwdriver storage rack, based on the size of half a standard sheet of pegboard. The size of the project can be varied to suit available space.**

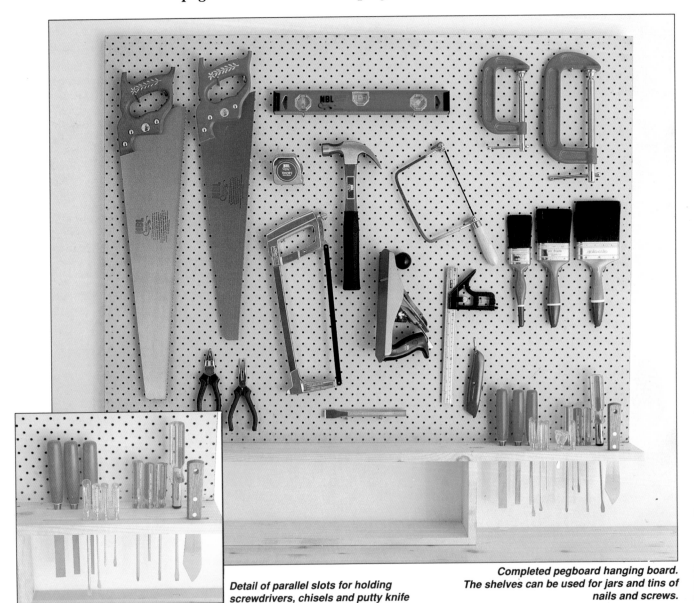

*Detail of parallel slots for holding screwdrivers, chisels and putty knife*

*Completed pegboard hanging board. The shelves can be used for jars and tins of nails and screws.*

## WHAT TO BUY

- [ ] 1 half sheet pre-primed 4.8 mm pegboard, 1830 mm x 1220 mm
- [ ] 50 mm x 25 mm PAR (planed all round) spruce, 1 of 4.8 m
- [ ] 150 mm x 25 mm PAR spruce, 1 of 2.4 m
- [ ] PVA adhesive
- [ ] handful of 25 mm round wire nails
- [ ] 17 of 40 mm 8 gauge countersunk screws
- [ ] 75 mm countersunk wood screws with cup washers for fixing to stud wall; and heavy-duty wallplugs for masonry walls
- [ ] assortment of pegboard hooks

## SPECIAL TOOLS NEEDED

- [ ] countersinking bit

## TIME

One day, plus painting if necessary

## STEP BY STEP

**1** Carefully check that the piece of pegboard you have is square, and sand the edges smooth. It should also have been cut between the holes (not through the holes).

**2** Measure the height, which should be 915 mm, and mark and cut two lengths of 50 mm x 25 mm spruce to this length.

**3** Using a small amount of PVA adhesive, nail lengths to the back sides of the pegboard.

**4** Measure the distance between the two side battens top and bottom, and cut to length two more lengths of 50 mm x 25 mm spruce.

**5** Apply PVA adhesive to each batten and its edges where it butts against the sides. Once again nail in place.

**6** Cut to length a piece of 150 mm x 25 mm spruce for the main shelf. This length should be 1220 mm the same as the length of the pegboard frame.

**7** Mark out a slot on the right-hand side of this shelf, 19 mm from the front edge and about 12 mm wide. This should stop 25 mm short of the right-hand edge and be 300 mm long.

**8** This can then be drilled for a starter hole, and then cut out using the jig saw.

**9** A second slot may be cut a further 50 mm back, if desired.

**10** The shelf can be screwed to the bottom of the pegboard frame using five 40 mm screws, and PVA adhesive.

**11** Cut two side panels for the shelf from the 150 mm x 25 mm spruce, 180 mm deep. Place the two ends together to ensure they are exactly the same length. One piece can be glued and screwed through the left-hand end of the shelf, and the other can be screwed through from the top of the shelf into the end piece, with its outside edge a distance of 850 mm from the left-hand side.

**12** Cut the bottom shelf to length. In this case it should be 812 mm. Glue and screw to the two side panels.

**13** The raw timber should be carefully sanded and then coated with two coats of polyurethane.

**14** The pegboard itself can be undercoated and painted with a gloss final coat, preferably using a pale colour, so that the outlines of the tools can be easily marked on the surface.

**15** You may care to screw (using two screws) several jam jar lids, or similar, to the underside of the bottom shelf for the storage of commonly used items such as screws, nails and pins. These items can be stored in the matching glass containers, which easily screw back into place.

**16** Using the 75 mm screws, find the studs and screw the completed project to the wall through the top and bottom battens behind the pegboard.

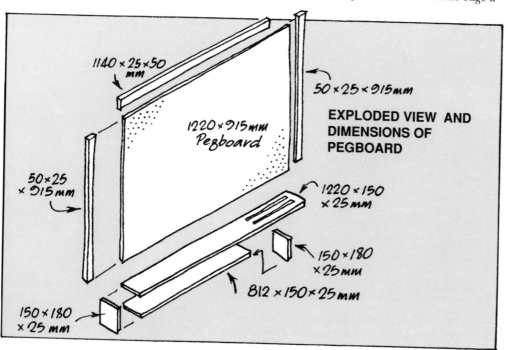

1140 × 25 × 50 mm

50 × 25 × 915 mm

1220 × 915 mm Pegboard

**EXPLODED VIEW AND DIMENSIONS OF PEGBOARD**

50 × 25 × 915 mm

1220 × 150 × 25 mm

150 × 180 × 25 mm

812 × 150 × 25 mm

150 × 180 × 25 mm

*Transporting tools safely*
*A tool carryall is excellent for the safe storage and transport of your tools and other small items (such as nails, hardware and adhesive) to and from a work area.*

*Project 2*

# Tool Carryall

The size and style of your carryall will be determined by where it is to be kept, the materials available and what you can carry. It's important that your carryall doesn't become a repository for junk. The carryall shown here is 500 mm long, by the planed width of a 200 mm x 25 mm board (190 mm plus 12 mm for two plywood sides) by 350 mm high.

*The completed tool carryall, in raw timber, well-stocked with basic tools*

*Using a bevel-edged chisel to form slots for tool storage*

## WHAT TO BUY

Normally a carryall is made of scrap timber left over from other projects or scavenged from elsewhere. However, a nice-looking new one can also be a work of art.

☐ 200 mm x 25 mm PAR spruce or similar, 1 of 1.2 m
☐ 38 mm x 25 mm PAR spruce or similar, 1 of 0.6 m
☐ 19 mm dowel hardwood, 1 of 0.6 m
☐ 600 mm x 400 mm x 6 mm plywood, 1 sheet
☐ round head wire nails 50 mm and 30 mm long
☐ PVA adhesive

## SPECIAL TOOLS NEEDED

☐ 19 mm flat bit and electric drill or 19 mm bit and brace

## TIME

Two to three hours

## STEP BY STEP

*1* Prepare a work space and lay out the materials.

*2* Square one end of the 200 mm x 25 mm board. Mark off 462 mm, the length of the carryall (500 mm) minus the thicknesses of the two ends (19 mm each). Square this and cut off the base, sawing on the waste side of the line.

*3* Similarly, mark and cut off two lengths of 350 mm of the board for the two end panels.

*4* On both end panels mark the centre of the hole for the handle halfway between the sides and 40 mm from the top. Bore a 19 mm diameter hole with a flat bit in an electric drill, or a brace and bit. If you only have a smaller bit, you will need to enlarge the hole with a round file. This will add some time to the project and can be quite frustrating.

*5* Mark off triangles to be removed from the top ends of the end panels. Measure 50 mm across the top of the end, and 110 mm down the side. Join the two points and cut off. Repeat this for all four top corners of the carryall.

*6* Cut two side panels of 500 mm x 180 mm out of the ply.

*7* Sand all edges using a sanding block to remove splinters.

*8* Apply a bead of PVA adhesive to one bottom end of the base and nail one end of the carryall to this using 50 mm nails. Repeat for the other side.

*9* Apply PVA adhesive to the side of the base and 180 mm up the edges of the end panels. Align and nail one plywood side in place using 30 mm nails. Repeat for the other side.

*10* Mark and cut to length the 19 mm diameter dowel. It is suggested the dowel protrude at either end a fraction and so is cut to a length of 550 mm. It should be a tight fit with no further fixing required. If loose, it can be held in place with a diagonally driven panel pin joining the dowel and the end panels.

*Nailing side of carryall to base*

*11* Mark and cut the 38 mm x 25 mm spruce (it should be 462 mm long) to fit between the two end panels along the inside top edge of one side. A series of 12 mm holes is drilled in this at 40 or 50 mm centres for storage of screwdrivers and small chisels, and joined 12 mm holes for wider tools such as wide chisels, rasps and files. This can be sanded smooth and fixed in place with PVA adhesive, nails from the ends and the plywood.

*12* Your carryall is now complete. Although it is normally left in raw timber it can be painted, stained or clear finished if desired.

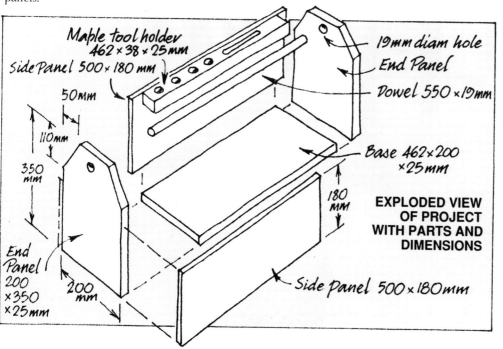

Maple tool holder 462 x 38 x 25mm
Side Panel 500 x 180 mm
50MM
110MM
350 mm
End Panel 200 x 350 x 25mm
200 mm
19mm diam hole
End Panel
Dowel 550 x 19mm
Base 462 x 200 x 25mm
180 MM
Side Panel 500 x 180mm

**EXPLODED VIEW OF PROJECT WITH PARTS AND DIMENSIONS**

**WALLS**

*Walls not only divide up different areas and define the space we live in – they also, quite literally, hold the roof over our heads and act as a major decorating feature in every room. Included here is a feast of inspiring ideas for walls and wallcoverings.*

# ALL ABOUT WALLS

## Clever ideas for the walls around you

*Wallpapered rendered walls with marbled architraves*

Lifestyle

**Some solid internal walls are load bearing – with a structural purpose, to hold up the roof of a building for example – and some are non-load-bearing. They may be there to divide up different areas, and to define interior and exterior space.**

Walls are often added or removed in the process of home improvement and to suit a growing family's changing needs. They may be made of stone, brick or block; or can be framed and panelled.

### REMOVING WALLS

If a wall is to be removed, it should first be carefully inspected to ensure it is not a structural element supporting another. In this case, if the wall is removed it could cause the structure to collapse. A wall may be holding up a vital section of the roof, an upper floor, or may act as a stiffener for an adjacent wall. The latter is especially important in terrace housing where you have no idea of what structural changes your neighbours have made.

If you don't feel competent enough to check the roofing structure and its support, get in a builder or building consultant to do the job. Before you do any work like this you should also check with your local building authority to ensure that you are allowed to do so.

*The versatility of plasterboard can be seen in this open-plan dining area*

Lifestyle

Lifestyle

*Floral-print wallpaper and matching drapes create a country-style feel*

Lifestyle

*Fibrous plaster walls with border to accent cornice*

*Opposite: Painted, rendered and set walls with an ornate cornice give this lounge room character*

Lifestyle

## BUILDING WALLS

New walls are often built to divide large rooms, or are built in the process of wall relocation.

Specifically, new walls may be used to divide a new en suite bathroom from a large bedroom, a bar from a lounge, or to divide a dormitory-style bedroom into two smaller, more private units.

When building a new room in this way, it is important that you allow sufficient light and ventilation for the purpose of the room so that the two divided areas still comply with any building regulations. Generally, 'habitable' rooms require window glass equal to at least 10 per cent of the floor area, and one half of that should afford good ventilation.

## MASONRY WALLS

Masonry walls are common in older full-brick buildings, but they are not so easily replaced once removed. Masonry walls are heavy (at least 0.25 tonnes to the square metre) and need correct support. They cannot just be built on an existing floor, but need to be taken to ground on a footing or a proper structural support such as a beam. An engineer should be commissioned to work out the minimum support needed in this case.

## FRAMED WALLS

Timber-framed walls are more common than masonry walls. Most home handypersons would build a timber-framed wall, which is then lined both sides with any number of materials. Most frames are 75 mm or 100 mm thick, with the lining adding a further 10 mm to 25 mm both sides. This should be taken into account when measuring up as 120 mm is an appreciable amount to lose in dividing spaces.

The frame is normally built to sit on the solid floor (not on the carpet) and fixed to the ceiling joists above. If the roof framing is of a truss type, the connection to the bottom binder of the roof truss should be flexible to allow for movement; the wall should not be a tight fit.

When building a new frame wall, it is a good opportunity to install extra services. A new switch layout, concealed telephone intercom wiring, or extra plumbing services can easily be incorporated into the wall.

## OTHER WALLS

There are other types of walls which you can build. Glass-block walls, for example, are designed to allow maximum light through. These can be heavy and you may need advice from an engineer about suspended locations. Glass blocks are also available in acrylic,

which are much lighter. Normally suppliers have detailed installation instructions for all of these.

Interior fixed glazing in either clear or obscured glass can also be used. There is no reason why office partitioning systems cannot also be used to divide rooms. These are generally metal-framed and modular and are best installed by the manufacturers.

If the 95 mm minimum wall thickness of a framed wall is excessive, another option is to use tongued and grooved particleboard (chipboard) of 19 mm thickness. This can be held bottom and top by fixed skirtings and covings

and, as long as the occasional vertical joint is not annoying, can provide a strong yet thin wall. Services are difficult to locate in this type of wall.

## WALL FINISHES

Once a wall has been built it can be finished in a myriad of ways. Painting and wallpapering on plasterboard or fibrous plaster are major possibilities, but other options exist. Decorative paint techniques are far more interesting than plain, painted walls – such as sponging and ragging paint finish techniques. Walls may be covered in fabrics and heavily textured weaves. Paintable fibreglass texture wall

coverings are available. Imitation suede is popular as are hessian finishes and cork tiles. In bathrooms, tiles are commonly used; but in other areas ceramic tiles, slate, marble, and granite are all possibilities. If you have lightweight walls but like the brick look, it is possible to adhere brick wafers to the wall to give a solid brick appearance.

Other possibilities are timber panelling which comes in a great variety of tonings and profiles, laminated sheets, and various plain and textured wallboards and vinyl linings.

The variety and possibilities are only limited by your imagination.

*Opposite: Sunny wallpapered bedroom walls with matching panels in doors to robe, hall and en suite*

*Open-plan living achieved by removing wall sections. Note the top of the wall in place to cover beam, and small nib walls for structural stability*

Lifestyle

*Changing needs*
*Somehow there never seems to be enough space at home, especially where children are involved. Changing needs often demand extra space and new interior layouts — how often have you wished you could push the walls apart just a fraction, add an extra room or wave a magic wand and conjure up more storage space?*

*Project 3*

# Dividing Wall

A wall frame is made of a number of parts. The main parts are plates, studs, heads, noggings, lintels and bracing.

**■ PLATES**
**Head plate:** The head plate forms the top of the wall. In this case, it supports no load other than wall linings.
**Sole plate:** The sole plate forms the bottom edge of the wall frame, and is supported by the floor frame.

Plates can be trenched to about 10 mm to allow for any difference in thickness. This is measured from the outside face of the plate to leave a uniform thickness on each plate. This is not necessary when plates are machine-gauged to a uniform thickness by the timber supplier.
**■ STUDS:** Studs are the vertical members between plates and can be spaced at 450 mm or 600 mm centres. To determine the length of the studs, measure the ceiling height and subtract the thicknesses of the plates.
**■ HEAD:** The door head is a horizontal short member above the door which in this case is not load bearing. If a head is load bearing, a lintel may be needed.

**This project consists of building a wall to divide a storage/pantry area from a dining room. It is 3.0 m long by the standard 2.4 m high. There is a doorway at one end to take a standard door. The wall framing must be solid, to provide fixing support for plasterboard on both sides as well as the door and door frame.**

*Completed wall covered in painted plasterboard with skirtings and architraves in place*

**4** Mark in the position of studs at the ends then space out and mark the studs at 450 mm centres. Allow for the thickness of the studs (50 mm). On these faces, mark which is the head and sole plate, and which way up they are to go.

**5** Measure the depth of the trenches or housings in the head and sole plates, and gauge them ready for cutting. The measurement should be taken from the top side of the head plate and bottom side of the sole plate. A maximum of 10 mm should be removed. A marking gauge can be used to mark the depth.

**6** Cut along the marks of the stud housings down to the gauged mark, then chisel out the housings with a 19 mm or 25 mm chisel and wooden mallet. Chisel from the centre of the housing towards the cuts, or from the edge to the centre. They can then be smoothed with a coarse rasp (make sure it has a handle). This whole procedure can be made easier with a power circular saw where the depth of cut is adjusted to a maximum of 10 mm and a series of parallel cuts are made between the marked housings. The residue left can be smoothed with the rasp if necessary. Professional frame carpenters use a radial-arm saw – this option is normally unavailable to home handypersons.

■ **NOGGINGS:** The studs in each wall are stiffened by the addition of noggings closely fitted between the studs. Noggings are usually the same size as the studs. They are placed approximately halfway between head and sole plates in walls up to 2700 mm in height.

■ **BRACING:** Occasionally walls must be stiffened against distortion by using diagonal bracing. This, however, is not common on interior dividing walls. The most effective angle for a brace is 45°. Bracing may be of timber or metal. Metal bracing should run in opposite directions.

■ **LINTELS:** Occasionally, where openings occur in the interior wall framing which also supports a roof, the load over the opening may be supported by a lintel.

## STEP BY STEP

*1* The wall will be built as one unit, and the studs will be housed into the head and sole plates. When completed it will be tilted into position and secured. It may be wise to make the frame about 10 mm short at the top to allow for wall variations and manoeuvring when putting in position.

*2* Lay out two straight timber lengths for plates on stools and hold them together with clamps. Mark and square the length, in this case 3000 mm minus 10 mm for ease of installation. Therefore total length will be 2990 mm. Cut to length.

*3* Mark the position for the door opening. The sole plate is left running through the door opening. This portion of the sole plate is not cut out until the wall is permanently fixed in position.

*Nailing noggings to studs*

*Securing bottom plate to floor along string line*

17

*Trueing studs prior to fixing to wall*

**7** Now calculate the length of the studs. The length will be 2400 mm minus an allowance for fitting of 10 mm, minus the remaining thickness of the two plates, which will be 40 mm each. The total length of the studs therefore is 2310 mm.

**8** Cut one stud to length then lay it between the head and sole plate on the floor. Check for total height to verify that all the measurements are correct.

**9** If the measurements are correct, cut the remaining five studs to length.

**10** Mark the door heads to provide an opening of 2100 mm in height on the two straightest studs. The mark will actually be 2060 mm from the base of the stud to allow for the thickness of the housed bottom plate. Mark a width of 50 mm, ready for housing in the head of the door, then cut and chisel out the housing.

**11** Now assemble the wall frames. Lay out the plates and studs on the floor as close as possible to where the wall frame is to go. Lay all the round edges of the studs the same way up.

**12** Nail the plates to the studs with two nails at each joint. This is easier with two people, one at each end.

**13** Cut to length the head over the door opening, which should be 900 mm plus 10 mm each end – that is, a total of 920 mm. Fit the head into the housings and nail into place.

**14** The noggings should be fixed with their centres about halfway between floor and ceiling. The noggings are fixed in a straight line or staggered. The noggings should not coincide with plasterboard joins.

**15** To fix the noggings, measure the length between studs and cut to length. Nail the noggings to the studs from each side along that line, stepping alternate noggings above and below the line.

**16** Cut and fit a short stud between head and head plate. This is about 210 mm long, and may possibly be an offcut from one of the plates, or from the noggings.

**17** Square up the wall frame by making the two diagonals equal by measuring with a steel tape. The diagonal should measure approximately 3842 mm. If the diagonals are not equal, adjust as necessary and then secure with a temporary diagonal brace.

**18** Carefully mark the position of the frame on the floor. It is worth double-checking this measurement. When satisfied, drive a 100 mm nail partly into the floor near both ends of the marked line to prevent the bottom plate of the frame from skidding beyond that point. Enlist some help when tilting frames into position to ensure a safe operation.

**19** When the frame has been stood upright, secure with a temporary nail into the wall until a more permanent fixing is made.

**20** The frame must now be trued accurately in a number of steps.

**21** Each end of the frame should be temporarily fixed to the floor on the mark previously made. It may be necessary to remove the temporary nail holding the frame to the wall to get it into the right position.

**22** Straighten the sole plate. Stretch a string line packed out from the sole plate using blocks of equal thickness. Align the sole plate to this and nail through into the joists if possible. If your wall is parallel to the joists, it may be worth installing a joist under the floor directly below the new wall.

**23** True the vertical of the two walls by using a plumb bob or a long level, then hold the frame in the vertical position with two nails. Place 'packing' between the existing walls and the new wall, and permanently nail the wall in place. On a brick wall three masonry bolts would be suitable. Suitable packing in this case would be plywood, fibre cement or hardboard offcuts.

**24** Check alignment of the head plate to a string line as for sole. Fix it to ceiling joists.

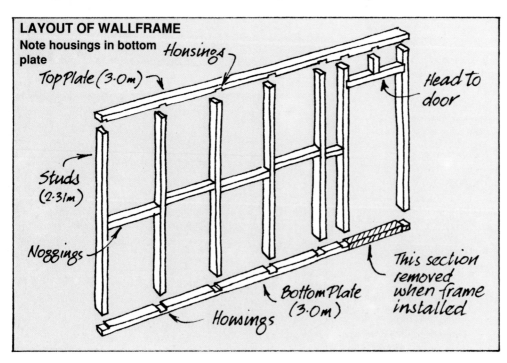

**LAYOUT OF WALLFRAME**
Note housings in bottom plate
Housings
Top Plate (3.0m)
Head to door
Studs (2.31m)
Noggings
Bottom Plate (3.0m)
Housings
This section removed when frame installed

*Finishing off*

*Our interior dividing wall, made from a framework of timber (see Project 3) has been built and is already in place. This frame is now ready to be lined (faced with plasterboard on both sides), finished off, and to have a door installed in it.*

*Project 4*

# Plasterboard and Cornices

**The wall is 3.0 m long by the standard 2.4 m high. We have allowed for a doorway at one end to take a standard door.**

We will fix 10 mm tapered-edge plasterboard to both sides; the joint to the ceiling will be finished without a cornice. Cornice-fixing details follow this basic plasterboard fixing guide.

As a general rule, it is in your interests to use as large a sheet size as can be reasonably handled, because this will eliminate joints and speed up the lining of the walls. The joints are to be set ready for finishing with either paint or wallpaper.

## STEP BY STEP

*1* Ensure that the walls are true and straight. Hold a long straight edge over the face of the studs and ensure there are no ridges or hollows. If a stud needs to be cut or straightened, use fish plates, as described in Tipstrip, to secure the cut. Otherwise, the studs will need to be shaved or packed to compensate.

*2* Make sure that there are no nails or other protuberances from the face of the studs.

*3* Any plumbing or wiring must be installed in the wall cavity before the plasterboard is fixed. You may prefer to leave this part of the job to

a professional rather than doing it yourself.

*4* Plasterboard can be fixed horizontally when using tapered-edge plasterboard.

*5* Mark the sheets to the correct size. The first sheet will only run as far as the door, so is cut 2050 mm. Mark the line to be cut on the face of the smaller sheet.

*6* Cut the sheet of plasterboard to size. This is most easily done using a sharp, short-bladed utility knife. Run the knife along the marked line using a straight edge of sufficient length. The board is then snapped back along this cut; the sheet will break and only be hinged by its rear paper.

*7* Cut through the rear paper face, from the rear, to separate the two sheets.

*8* Place two offcuts of 10 mm plasterboard on the floor at the base of the wall to automatically give the required gap to the floor.

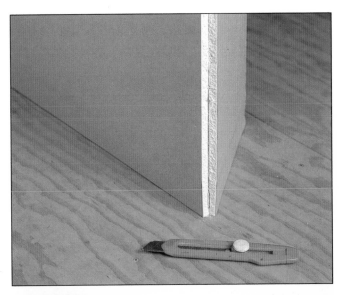

*Plasterboard adhered and nailed in place*

*Top: Using utility knife to cut plasterboard*

*Applying jointing cement and bottom tape to recessed sheet joint*

**9** Apply the plasterboard adhesive to the studs so that they will not coincide with the nailing positions of the sheets. The adhesive should be applied in dobs about the size of a 10p coin.

**10** Fit the plasterboard to the wall and secure with galvanised plasterboard nails. Nailing should be at every stud. The sheets should be nailed about 12 mm from the edge and again in the centre of the sheet on each stud. Double-nail with the second nail about 60-75 mm away from the first to properly secure the wall. The manufacturers recommend that you don't nail to the noggings.

**11** The second sheet will need to be fitted around the door and over its top. This should be carefully measured, and marked on the face of the sheet.

**12** To cut a rectangle out of a corner of the board, the first shorter cut can be made with a panel saw, and the second cut with the utility knife – snapping the sheet as before.

**13** When cut, fit the second sheet over the first. Manoeuvring the sheet into position in a tight space can be tricky and it is important that it is lifted straight without skewing, as this may damage adjacent wall linings

and the corners of the sheet itself. A second person would certainly be a help!

**14** When the sheet is in position, adhere and nail it in place as before.

**15** Cut a narrow strip and fit in place down the remaining stud at the door, to even out the face for future application of the architraves of the door.

**16** Now the joints are ready to be set for a smooth finish. Firstly ensure there are no

dust or other contaminants on the sheets by wiping them over with a damp cloth.

**17** Apply self-adhesive scrim tape to the joint and firm it in place as you go.

**18** This tape is then covered with a good layer of jointing plaster applied with the filling knife to a width of about 100 mm to 150 mm. This should be finished to the level of the surrounding plasterboard, and not be built up to a higher level.

**19** Similarly the joint to the ceiling must be taped and set but in this case using an internal corner finishing tool. The tape is firmly pushed into the corner, and for each layer of plaster applied to the face of the plasterboard, a layer of finishing plaster is applied to the corner and worked in position using the corner finishing tool.

**20** After 24 hours, when the first application of jointing plaster is dry, the second can be applied, slightly wider to say 200 mm, being careful to

apply it as smoothly to the level of plasterboard as possible.

**21** This is also let to dry, and the final application of jointing plaster is applied in a broad band about 250 mm in width to achieve a completely smooth joint, that is completely flush with the plasterboard surrounds. For an even finer edge, it can be gently brushed with a damp brush to completely 'feather' the edge.

## FINISHING THE WALL
Having finished the plasterwork, the wall can be prepared for painting or wallpapering. If you are using natural timber skirting boards it may be worthwhile to fix them after the wall has been painted.

The paper face of plasterboard is quite absorbent, and the jointing cement will have a different suction to the face of the boards. It is recommended that you first seal the surface with a wallboard sealer, which

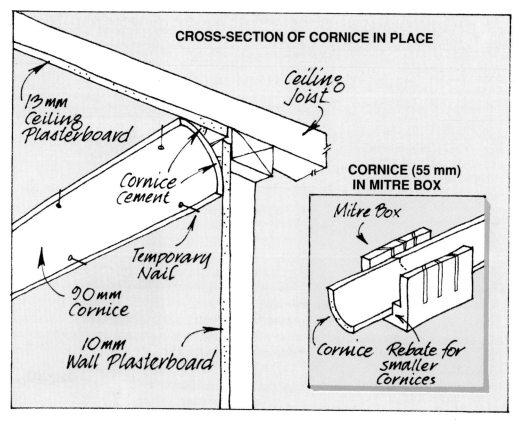

CROSS-SECTION OF CORNICE IN PLACE

Ceiling Joist

13 mm Ceiling Plasterboard

Cornice Cement

Temporary Nail

90 mm Cornice

10 mm Wall Plasterboard

CORNICE (55 mm) IN MITRE BOX

Mitre Box

Cornice Rebate for smaller Cornices

may be either acrylic or oil based.

Sealers are simply painted or rolled on. Allow to dry between 4 and 24 hours depending on the product used. At this stage the wall may be papered or painted. Our example was painted using two coats of a quality water-based, low-sheen vinyl paint. The edges and cutting-in were done with a 50 mm brush, and the wall then generally coated with a roller (fine-to-medium nap). Painting walls with oil-based paints is more involved and the clean-up is nowhere near as easy.

For wallpapering, the surface is coated with size, and then papered with any of the vast range of papers on the market. For first-time wallpaperers, pre-pasted paper is easiest to use.

Coat the skirting boards and the architraves around the door with a coat of polyurethane. When dry, fix the skirting boards firstly to the doorway, and then around the bottom of the floor. Skirting boards are scribed rather than mitred into the corners. They can be nailed to the base of the wall because there is a structural timber member, the sole

plate, behind there. When fixed, the nails can be punched below the surface, and the holes filled with a matching wood-stopping compound. The final coat of polyurethane is applied to finish off the room.

## CORNICES

A cornice is a continuous horizontal plaster moulding, often quite ornate and decorative, at the joint of wall and ceiling.

*1* If cornices are to be fitted to the ceiling and wall junction, mark down the wall in several places along its length, and join the marks to indicate where the bottom of the cornice will be.

*2* Measure the lengths of the cornice required. It is a good idea to cut the long length about 3 mm oversize so that it can be snapped into position, forming a tight joint.

*3* Use a mitre box to cut a mitre at both ends of the long and short lengths. Make sure that the mitre runs the correct way – the two lengths should be a mirror image of each other. Where the cornice needs to be joined, cut the mitres before they are

cut to length. This will allow you more choices in case of an error.

*4* Install the shorter lengths first.

*5* Mix the cornice plaster with water to a creamy consistency. The mixture is useable for about 30 minutes.

*6* Butter 10 mm beads of cornice plaster on the back of the cornice edges. Apply cornice plaster to one length at a time, and fix that length in place. On a hot day it may be worth slightly dampening the cornice where the plaster is applied to stop it drying out too quickly.

*7* Put each short piece in position and hold in place using some temporary nails; if in doubt about their holding in place, use galvanised nails about 25 mm in from the edge nailed into the frame.

*8* When in place, butter the long length and, bending slightly, 'snap' it into place. Once again hold it firmly in place with galvanised nails.

*9* As the cornice plaster goes off rather quickly, it is important to clean off all excess plaster at the earliest possible time.

*10* When set, apply finishing plaster to the mitres. Finish off the joint with a light brush-over with a damp brush to smooth the joint.

*11* Remove all temporary nails. Apply a second coat of filler to the mitres and joints as well as to the nail holes. Use the damp brush again for a feather edge.

*12* When all is set, a light sanding using #150 grade paper with a float on the flat areas and by hand on the curved, will leave a surface ready for sealing for paint or wallpaper.

*One of the most attractive feature walls is one lined with a beautifully grained and coloured species of timber. Solid timber panelling is available in many species all of which have their own charm. The timbers may be local or imported.*

*Project 5*

# Timber Panelling

**P**anelling is normally solid timber, but a large range of decorative plywoods and other boards are available, with exotic species of timber in veneer form. The price for all types of panelling will vary greatly, depending mainly on the species and thickness of timber used.

The profile may be shiplap, where one board overlaps another, or be tongue and grooved (t & g), where each board has a milled tongue which fits into the groove of the next board. These are often milled to give a V-joint. Some shiplap profiles also feature t & g grooves for secret fixing or reversal of the timber to provide a t & g finish.

**Our project is the timber panelling of a staircase. The staircase has four risers to a landing and then a further nine risers to the upstairs area. The timber selected for the panelling is Western red cedar. However, any other timber can be used. The profile is a 150 mm shiplap suitable for secret nailing. Because of the profile the effective cover is only 133 mm.**

*Timber feature wall*

*Additional noggings ready to be fixed to frame*

## STEP BY STEP

**1** Before putting up panelling it is essential to ensure that the wall is plumb and straight. Timber panelling that is 12 mm thick will follow any irregularities in the wall. If the wall is irregular, grounds may need to be built and fixed, and packed to provide a plumb and straight base (see Tipstrip).

**2** Timber panelling must be properly supported to avoid distortion or breakage. Intermediate noggings should be fitted between timber studs so that the maximum unsupported length of the panel is 600 mm.

**3** Panelling must be straight to look effective! We will start over the doorway, and work down the stairs. Once the wall has been checked and prepared as necessary, it is time to mark in a true vertical line near one corner of the wall. Unless the adjoining wall is perfectly true and plumb, this mark should be slightly less than the width of the panelling timber profile. This allows the board to be scribed to the corner.

**4** Using a long level or a plumb line, mark a true vertical on each nogging from this mark.

**5** Temporarily, fix the panel along the vertical line, with the tongue facing away from the wall. Two panel pins only partly driven should be plenty.

**6** Transfer the profile of the wall onto the panel, by running a short offcut down the wall together with a sharp pencil marking the outline of the wall on the timber length that was fixed temporarily. Extract the nails, and the board can then be taken away and planed to the marked line, which is the exact shape that will fit the adjacent wall.

**7** The first panel can then be nailed to the wall. Most profiles are milled to allow for secret nailing, so that nail heads are not visible. Use only fine panel pins to avoid the problem of timber splitting, and place the nail where the next panel will cover the nail head.

**8** With all panelling, it is wise to hammer the nail only to within about 3 mm of the surface, after which the nail should be driven with the aid of a nail punch. Western red cedar marks easily and hammer marks all over the wall are most unattractive.

**9** The next length will only need to be cut to length. It is then fitted with its grooves properly engaged in the tongue of the first panel. This

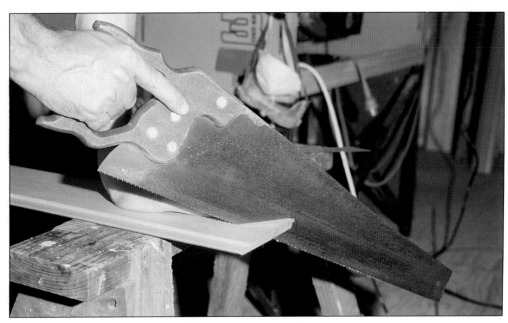

*Cutting panels at an angle for the staircase*

■ Where walls are not suitable to have the timber applied directly due to irregularities or bowing or hollows, a separate frame will need to be made first. This frame is called the ground. Grounds can be fabricated and fixed to the wall, or can be built directly onto the wall. They are normally made of 50 mm x 25 mm softwood. The important dimension is the thickness, as this ensures a smooth wall. Grounds can be nailed to the studs of timber-framed walls or can be stuck or fixed with frame fixings to brickwork. If the walls are uneven, it may be necessary to pack behind them to bring them level.

■ If you wish to fix the timber panelling in the horizontal plane or even diagonally, the battens will have to be repositioned to ensure that adequate fixing is available. Horizontal panelling can be directly attached to the framework of the house, as studs occur every 450 mm or 500 mm.

■ Traditionally, timber panelling was fixed to frames by nailing directly. Some timber suppliers strongly suggest both nailing and gluing with a good-quality wallboard adhesive for the best results.

■ If using plywood, a variety of finishes and colours are available. Fixing plywood is very similar, with similar requirements for support. Plywood for walls usually has a regular or random-groove pattern, and the nails are easily disguised if hammered in the grooves.

can be tight at times, and you may need to tap the board into place. If you just use a hammer, the timber edge will be crushed and distorted, and the next panel will be difficult to fit. Tapping into place is best done using an offcut of the panel, and snapping it in half along its grain. This will give you a grooved half that can be fitted over the tongue and used as a hammering block. It will not damage the delicate edges of the panelling.

**10** Slowly begin fixing the panelling to the wall, checking every two or three boards to make sure that the panelling is still truly vertical.

**11** After six lengths of panelling are fitted over the door, the next will need to be cut out around the door. Cut a board to the total height of

*Panel moved to show nailing position for 'secret nailing'*

floor to ceiling, and then hold it against the door and mark off the top of the jamb. Fit another small offcut into the tongue of the board last fitted and mark the width of the cut on the offcut. This

*Using level to plumb panels*

can be accurately transferred to the new length you are preparing.

**12** To cut the section out, use your panel saw and cut along the grain first. This is called ripping. Do this gently, as timbers with a well-defined grain can easily split along the grain rather than the mark if the saw is forced. At the marked end, cut off across the grain.

**13** When fitting this panel take extra care to get the board truly plumb.

**14** The following panels start going down the stairs, and each will be longer than the preceding one. To get the angle right, set a sliding bevel permanently to the angle between the top of the stair string and a true vertical. This technique will always give you the right angle at which to mark and cut the bottom of each panel. As you proceed down the stairs, you will need a ladder to reach the higher areas to effectively nail the timber in position. A small extension ladder is ideal, together with a ladder leveller so that you can use it on the stairs. Each top point of the ladder should be well wrapped in foam rubber, and then in an old cloth. This way you can work safely without marking the panelling with the ladder. Don't balance the ladder on boxes or bricks – they are not safe.

**15** When you are about two or three boards from the end of the wall, put them into position, without nailing. You will have to measure the final board to trim it to shape. This is easiest when the adjacent boards are not fixed. In some cases it may be necessary to round off the back of the final board so that it can be slipped into the corner.

**16** When the panel is an exact fit, fix all the last panels into position. This includes those on opposite walls.

**17** There will be one external angle on the landing. This can be dressed by using a specially moulded corner piece in the same timber.

**18** At this stage, it is time to start applying all the trim pieces such as architraves around the door, beads to cover joints between balustrading bottom rails and panelling, and to the stair strings where necessary.

**19** It is also time to apply the brackets to fix the handrail section. These cannot be supported by the timber panelling, and must be fixed through to the studs behind the panelling.

**20** Finishing of timber panelling is up to you. Most people prefer to use low-sheen finishes and these can be achieved using the various finishing oils on the market. If the panelling is likely to undergo frequent handling, a polyurethane will be the easiest surface to wipe down. Regardless of which is chosen for the panelling, the staircase and strings should be coated in a hard-wearing finish such as polyurethane because of the wear it will be subjected to.

Lifestyle

## STRUCTURE OF TIMBER-PANELLED STAIRCASE

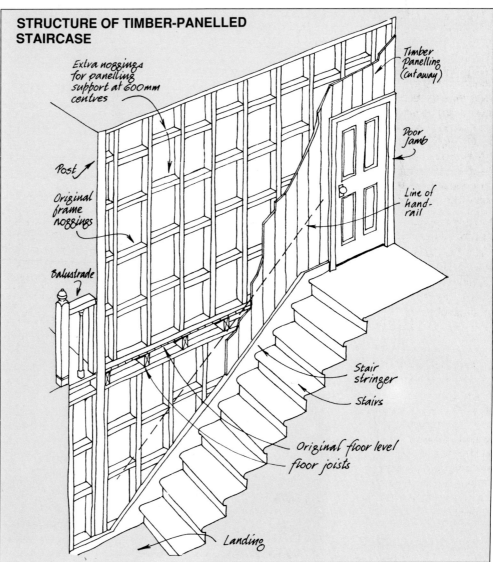

Extra noggings for panelling support at 600mm centres

Timber Panelling (cutaway)

Post

Original frame noggings

Door Jamb

Line of hand-rail

Balustrade

Stair stringer

Stairs

Original floor level

floor joists

Landing

*In recent times, the bathroom has become more and more the glamour room of the house, with a wealth of fittings, fixtures and accessories. It can also be the most difficult room to decorate because it is often small, and must be waterproof, properly drained and ventilated to ensure no long-term problems. Bathroom surfaces are an important practical feature, and are especially high on the home improvements list.*

*Project 6*

# Bathroom Tiling

The bathrooms in older homes were often lined in a pre-finished sheeting. In our bathroom renovation project, the walls are to be tiled to the ceiling. The tiling will have to be fixed around a spa bath as well.

*Tiling completed and grouted over spa bath*

## WHAT TO BUY

- ☐ 6 mm Masterboard sheets
  - 1 of 900mm x 1800 mm
  - 3 of 1200 mm x 1800 mm
  - 1 of 1200 mm x 3000 mm
  - 1 of 1200 mm x 2400 mm
- ☐ galvanised 38 mm x No 8 countersunk screws
- ☐ wallboard adhesive
- ☐ 27 sq.m of 300 mm x 150 mm tiles
- ☐ tile wall adhesive
- ☐ white compressible grout

## SPECIAL TOOLS NEEDED

- ☐ notched trowel
- ☐ spatula or straight-edged float
- ☐ rubber squeegee
- ☐ tungsten-tipped tile pincers
- ☐ tungsten-tipped tile cutter (hire)
- ☐ tungsten carbide rod saw and frame (if necessary)
- ☐ spare cloths
- ☐ bucket
- ☐ sponge

## TIME

Two weekends, plus one or two following nights

In preparation for tiling, the shower screen will have to be removed, as well as the vanity unit, the wall taps and the shower rose in the shower.

Our bathroom is 3000 mm x 2650 mm, and the shower recess is 900 mm x 950 mm. The total area for tiling is about 25.2 sq.m, but allow 27 sq.m for cutting, safety and for spares.

## STEP BY STEP

*1* Carefully measure up all surfaces in the room. Make a rough diagram of each wall, and the area of tiles required for each wall.

*2* Remove old sheets. These were probably screwed into place so will need to be unscrewed. They are not reuseable. Don't smash them up as they may contain a small amount of asbestos fibre. This should be dealt with using the correct disposal methods applicable in your area. The aluminium joining strips should also be removed and discarded.

*3* The shower recess will need to have a properly installed shower tray. This must be sealed to the floor waste and turned at least 150 mm up the wall. Special attention needs to be paid to the hob area. The wall sheet should lap down over the upturns of the shower tray.

*4* Line the walls with sheets of Masterboard with the rough side facing out. This is a highly suitable surface to tile. Leave a slight gap between sheets to allow for expansion and contraction. Fixing should be at 300 mm centres to each stud and noggings. Use countersunk screws and make sure the heads are below the surface. The use of a wallboard

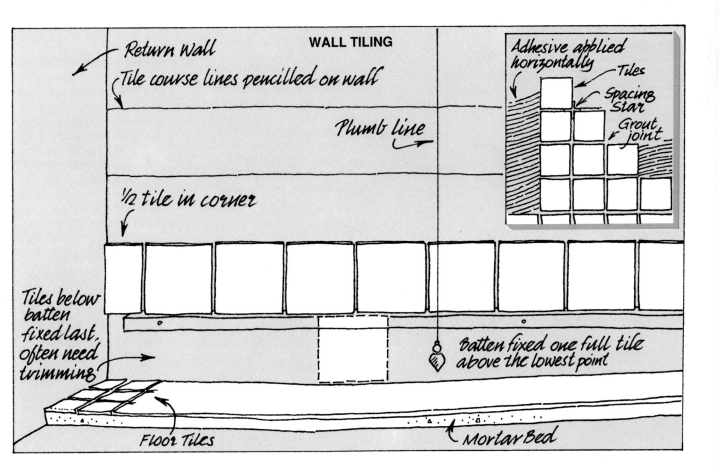

**WALL TILING**

Return Wall

Tile course lines pencilled on wall

Plumb line

Adhesive applied horizontally — Tiles

Spacing Star

Grout joint

½ tile in corner

Tiles below batten fixed last, often need trimming

Batten fixed one full tile above the lowest point

Floor Tiles

Mortar Bed

**Shower recess sheets installed over copper shower tray**

**Cutting tiles**

adhesive between the sheets and the studs will further strengthen the wall substrate.

**5** Prime the Masterboard sheets with a PVA-based ceramic tiling primer, or as recommended by the adhesive manufacturer (must be suitable for binding the dust of the sheets).

**6** Find the lowest point of the floor on each wall; then select the lowest of these. This is your starting level. Mark one tile height at this lowest point.

**7** Level right around the room at this level using your 900 mm level.

**8** Nail thin straight battens right around the room with the top edge of the batten coinciding with the mark. Once again, check that the batten is level, otherwise it will completely throw the tiling out.

**9** Find the centre of each wall, and with a plumb line mark a true vertical at the exact centre.

**10** Loosely lay out the tiles on the batten, allowing at least a 3 mm gap between tiles with a joint at the middle mark (grout joint). It is desirable and easier to have half tiles at each end rather than having to remove a thin sliver, or worse still have to cut a thin sliver at each end. If necessary, move the tiles so that the centre of the wall corresponds with the centre of a tile. The reason for doing all of this is that the wall corner may not be entirely square.

**11** Next, mark out the vertical height of each course of tiles on a separate piece of batten and, again, 3 mm grout joints. Hold this on the bottom batten, and make sure that the tiling will finish where you want it to. If it does not and you want a full tile at the top, you may have to drop the bottom batten correspondingly to get the right effect.

**12** It is worth spending a considerable amount of time getting the set-out right. Once you are happy with the layout, mark the position of each tile on the batten and pencil in a few more straight vertical lines corresponding with the tile joints. All the tiles, other than those that need to be cut at the floor and the sides, will be full tiles. You are now ready to apply the tiles.

**13** Read the instructions on the adhesive container. In this case we are using PVA adhesive which requires no mixing, sets relatively quickly, and is simple to use. It is suitable for most surfaces. Only apply enough adhesive to lay 1 sq.m of tiles at a time (maximum). This will ensure that the adhesive does not 'skin' over and have poor adhesion.

**14** The starting point is the middle of the wall. Work to one side – the bathroom walls are small enough to work right into one edge, barring the cut tile.

**15** Apply the adhesive with a spatula or a straight-edged float to cover the tiling area. When covered, hold a 4.5 mm notched trowel edge-on and notch the adhesive horizontally across the area. Some people prefer to load adhesive directly onto the notched trowel and then work it onto the wall. Use whichever method you find easiest.

**16** Place the tiles into position on the wall and bed them with a slight twisting motion, allowing for grouting joints. Tile spacers may be used to achieve the right grout gap. The whole of the back of the tile must be in contact with the adhesive. To this end it is desirable to occasionally remove a tile that has just been positioned to ensure that complete coverage is indeed being achieved.

**17** Any excess adhesive should be removed from the face of the tiles with a damp cloth as tiling progresses. If a coloured grout is being used the adhesive should be removed to below the face level of the tiles, otherwise white adhesive may show through in patches. Also, as the adhesive holds the tiles in place, any spacers should also be removed.

**18** Check your progress frequently with a level and to the lines you have drawn on the wall.

**19** Leave any cut tiles to the end. This includes the bottom and the side tiles. It also includes tiles that need to be cut around the bath, tap fittings, or any special-purpose tiles such as the soap-holder or towel rail bracket tiles. Make sure you scrape any excess adhesive from these areas while it is still soft.

**20** After 12 hours the bottom battens can be removed.

**21** The tiles will need to be cut straight around the floor and sides. To mark the cut, place a full tile exactly over the last tile laid and push a second tile over its face against the wall. Make an allowance for the grout joint. Mark this line.

**22** Place the tile on a tile cutter, align the mark with the wheel, scribe, and then press the handle down to snap the tile. Alternatively, place the tile to be cut on a firm base and, using another tile or a straight edge, score the glazed surface with a tungsten-tipped tile cutter. Place a small nail under one end of the score mark, and firmly press the tile down. The tile will snap right along your scribed line. The cut edge can be smoothed by rubbing it on some concrete or an abrasive stone. As you cut the tiles, adhere them into the correct position to avoid any mix-ups later.

**23** Tiles that are to be fitted around tap holes need to have a curved section cut out. Mark out the curve, allowing at least 5 mm clearance to the metalwork. This can be done patiently by scoring the required curve and slowly

*Grouting the tiles*

snapping off small pieces with tungsten-tipped tile pincers. An alternative is to use a tungsten carbide-charged rod saw that fits into either a coping saw or hacksaw frame and can be used to cut out the curve.

**24** At this time, also install any soap-holder and towel rail brackets. Make sure you install the rod in the brackets before the second bracket is set in place. Cover these fittings well with adhesive and hold in place with masking tape for 24 hours.

**25** Allow the tiling to cure for at least 24 hours, and then the joints can be grouted.

**26** Mix the grout as per manufacturer's specifications and let stand for a few minutes. Apply the grout with a rubber squeegee diagonally in both directions across the tiles. Do small areas at a time. When the grout is in place the joint may be more firmly packed by running over it with a length of dowelling or similar. Gently rub off the excess with a slightly dampened sponge, washing frequently. Make sure you clean the area before the grout sets.

**27** When the surface is dry only a faint grout stain should be visible on the surface of the tiles. This can be polished off with a clean cloth.

**28** The wall tiles will be properly set after a further 24 hours.

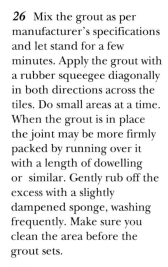

*An attractive bathroom can be made using tiles in wet and splash areas, and a durable timber coated with polyurethane. Note that in this case the floor has been laid diagonally*

## TIPSTRIP

### MEASURING UP
Measure the area to be tiled and calculate the number of tiles you will need. Most suppliers will tell you the number of tiles needed per square metre. Your measurements should be accurate and in square metres. It pays to buy about 5 per cent more tiles than you need, to allow for breakages. Allow for edging and corner tiles if these are available.

### ADHESIVE
When using adhesives, never wet the tiles prior to laying.

Don't notch the adhesive vertically as any water penetrating the grout joints of the finished tiling will then run down the wall and collect at the bottom (rather than being held at the level of penetration where there will be a larger area for evaporation).

### ASBESTOS
Any material that is suspected of containing asbestos should be removed and disposed of in accordance with any regulations in force in your area, or methods recommended by the health department.

### TILE SPACERS
Don't rely on the tiny spacer lugs present on the sides of many tiles to provide the grouting joint. The lug is designed to crush if the tiles expand; but experience has shown this generally does not occur – with the result that in large areas of tiling the wall tiles come loose. It is better to use nylon spacers or matchsticks. Do not use nails.

*Windows are a major visual feature of the modern house, they are also its eyes – imparting style, character and personality while providing good ventilation and light.*

# LET IN THE LIGHT

## Bright ideas for light and shade

*This skylight opens out and brightens up an otherwise dark and featureless hallway*

*Australian Colonial Federation style windows to a dining room*

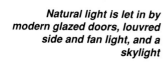

*Natural light is let in by modern glazed doors, louvred side and fan light, and a skylight*

*Opposite: Lounge with French doors and windows with colonial glazing bars, and featuring a section of glazed roof*

Lifestyle

Lifestyle

*French leadlight doors are a feature of this living area, adding their own distinctive, very decorative character*

O penings in houses may be voids, doors or windows. Voids tend to be in areas where security is not a consideration, such as between rooms in an open-plan living area. Doors provide a means of access and security to the building. Windows, however, are designed to provide daylight and a means of ventilation. They should also provide a view, but still allow for privacy when required.

The difficulty in placing windows is that the best position for maximum daylight may not coincide with the best view, or best ventilation possible. Compromises are inevitable. The light admitted will depend not only on position but also on the type of glass used, the reflection from walls, floor and ceilings; and the sun control treatment used.

## GLASS

Glass in most instances will be clear. However, for areas such as bathrooms, glass is available in various levels of obscurity, or it may be tinted. The range of solar and reflective glasses, although expensive, may be used to control solar radiation. Safety glass should be used around sliding doors and floor-level glazing panels.

## WINDOWS

There are many types of windows, each with their advantages and disadvantages.

**Fixed windows:** Don't have any opening sashes. They are not normally used as the only window in a room.

**Timber sash (box-framed) windows:** The old traditional windows where the sashes slide up and down, and are counterbalanced by weights.

**Casement windows:** Style where the sash is hinged on the vertical framing members.

**Double-hung windows:** The modern equivalent of the old timber sash window. Both top and bottom open to allow convection movement of air.

**Sliding windows:** Commonly aluminium, where one half slides past the other fixed half. This allows large, open areas.

**Awning (top-hung) windows:** Style where the sash is hinged to the top horizontal member and opens out. They may be left open in the rain, but allow only limited air circulation.

**Sashless windows:** Glass without a frame, various styles but mainly for commercial purposes.

Frame materials may be timber, aluminium, steel or PVC. The choice will be based on the style of house, exposure, availability, and maintenance requirements.

## LEADLIGHTS

An attractive alternative is leadlight or stained glass. These are available as 'standard' panels or a leadlight, or stained glass panel can be commissioned from an artist. Imitation leadlighting with surface-applied lead and a stain wash to the glass is also available.

## GLASS BRICKS

Glass bricks are a way of providing obscured filtered light into areas such as stairwells and bathrooms. Their installation is exacting, and allowance must be made for expansion and contraction.

## PATIO DOORS

Patio doors are an extension of multiple windows, and in many homes may be a combination of normal opening floor-to-ceiling windows, together with fixed sashes. For ventilation in humid situations, banks of louvres may be used.

## CONSERVATORIES

Conservatories are a popular extension of patio doors, where the roof or part of the roof is also glazed. It is important to use a proprietary system and keep the pitch correct, to achieve adequate waterproofing.

## SKYLIGHTS

Where rooms are enclosed and don't have their own window, a common option is that of a skylight or roof 'window'. They are effective together with a lightwell, and are available in vented or unvented styles.

*Attic room with both dormer window and a double-glazed roof window*

Barrel lights may have curved glass and glazing bars and can be made to cover entire rooms. It is important in this case to watch the heat gain through the glazing – many people find air-conditioning a necessity after installation.

## SHADING

Shading of windows is possible in many ways. Most effective are external methods such as awnings, external blinds and louvres or shutters. Also effective are solar films. On the interior, heat can be controlled with reflective blinds and a range of venetians, blinds, and even curtains.

*A rather beautiful entrance, with its timber-strip floor, well-chosen antiques and understated decor, is highlighted even more by a large skylight*

*Skylights and roof windows can help to transform any room, especially those with little access to natural light.*

# Installing a Skylight

## STEP BY STEP

*1* The size of a skylight is based on the floor area of the area to be lit. It is generally recommended that the skylight be at least 10 per cent of the floor area. In this case the skylight will be 800 mm x 800 mm.

*2* Order the skylight, specifying size, roof type, the shape required, and if any accessories, such as diffusers or solar control features are required.

*3* Climb into the roof space to decide where the skylight is to go.

*4* Remove tiles and sarking felt in the area where the skylight is to be installed. Treat the tiles carefully as some will be needed later. Stack them to one side.

*5* Carefully mark on the rafters and battens where the skylight is to go. Make a 50 mm allowance top and bottom of the rafter for the trimmers which are needed to frame the cut-out hole. This should be done with reference to the ceiling and where the lightwell is to go. Also take note of any wires, pipes, roof ridges or valleys that may affect the installation, or will require moving.

The project is to install a skylight in a concrete tile roof to provide a lightwell for maximum lighting in an enclosed kitchen. The skylight will be 800 mm square so will need a rafter cut, and the lightwell is to be painted white for maximum natural light.

**Completed skylight in kitchen**

**Tiles removed from roof**

**6** Cut the battens flush with the rafters, and nail any loose trimmed battens to the rafters. Make sure no battens run across the area in which the skylight is to be installed.

**7** There is a bend in the tray of the skylight and this should be in line with the bottom edge of the batten.

**8** As this is a wide model, it will be necessary to saw through one rafter at the top and bottom of the cut-out. Do this carefully to the marks, making sure you have made an allowance for the thickness of the trimmer top and bottom.

**9** Cut two trimmers to length, top and bottom, to secure the cut rafter. The trimmer should be a tight fit between the two adjacent rafters. Measure the trimmer directly. When nailing it in place ensure that it is completely square to the rafter and truly horizontal using a level. A short length of rafter will be needed between the trimmers to allow for the width of the skylight.

**10** Remove the internal catches that hold the dome of the skylight to its base. In most cases these will be internal toggle catches.

**11** Place the base over the opening. Make sure that the joint where the flashing joins onto the base is supported by a tile.

**12** Secure the anchoring straps of the base to rafters by nails or screws.

**13** Make sure that all the folds and channels on the base have not been deformed as this could affect the waterproofing of the skylight, especially in high winds.

**14** Re-lay the tiles to within 50 mm of the vertical side upstands of the base. (To do this with terracotta tiles it may be necessary to remove the lugs from the underside of the tiles.)

**15** Dress the lead flashing over the lower tiles. In high-exposure areas, point up with cement mortar between the lead and tiles. This should not, however, normally be necessary.

**16** As we are also fitting a lightwell it may be easier to leave the dome until the lightwell is installed. Usually the dome would be fitted into position as recommended by the manufacturer and the toggles replaced and firmly sealed from the inside.

**17** The lightwell can be flared to be wider at the ceiling than at the skylight. This will give a better distribution of light in the room. However, keep the lightwell between the matching ceiling joists and expand it in the other direction, otherwise large trimming joists will be needed to support the ceiling

**Trimmers installed and battens secured**

adequately – especially if the ceiling is a large one.

**18** Measure down to the ceiling where it is to be cut. Mark on the ceiling rafters the position of the lightwell. Drive a nail through the ceiling lining to mark each corner of the lightwell on the underside of the ceiling

where the cuts are to be made.

**19** Make sure that there are no electric wires, telephone wires or plumbing pipes in the lightwell area before cutting.

**20** Mark out the rectangle to be cut on the ceiling on the room side.

*Dressing lead to the tiles*

*Base of skylight and tiles back in place*

**21** Cut the ceiling lining to the marks with a panel saw. As it is plaster it should be easy to cut but, if working from below, wear goggles and a face mask to protect the eyes and breathing passages against plaster dust.

**22** Install the trimming joists for the ceiling, once again making sure that the opening is framed square.

**23** The simplest method of lightwell construction, where the distance between roof rafter and ceiling joist is not great, is to make the well out of chipboard or medium density fibreboard. This is carefully marked out to the shape required, and prefabricated using adhesive and nailing, before being fitted.

**24** This is then lifted into place from the underside of the ceiling, and nailed in place.

**25** It is finished with a timber trim to cover the joint to the ceiling.

*Inserting prefabricated lightwell*

**26** As an alternative, the lightwell can be framed between the roof rafters and the ceiling joists. This is best made of 75 mm x 38 mm softwood framing. The job will be greatly simplified with the use of nail plates to enable you to build the box on top of the ceiling joists, and directly under the roof rafters. You will, however, find that due to the construction of the roof they will be offset by the thickness of a roof rafter. Remember to design the framing with corners so that you have something to fix the lining of the lightwell to. When the frame is secure the lightwell can be lined. It is best to use a 'warm' material as this will have greater resistance to condensation. Timber linings are excellent, but foil-backed plasterboard, chipboard or plywood would also suffice. A high level of finish is not required to the lightwell if it is hidden behind a diffuser. However, if there is no diffuser, greater care will be needed in finishing off.

**27** Finish the interior of the lightwell with two or three coats of white vinyl paint.

**28** A diffuser panel can be loosely fitted on top of neat timber battens nailed to the sides of the lightwell, flush to 50 mm from the ceiling level. These should be installed prepainted.

**29** Fit the diffuser by passing it up at an angle and twisting it and lowering it into position.

*Nailing cleats for a neat lightwell to ceiling joint*

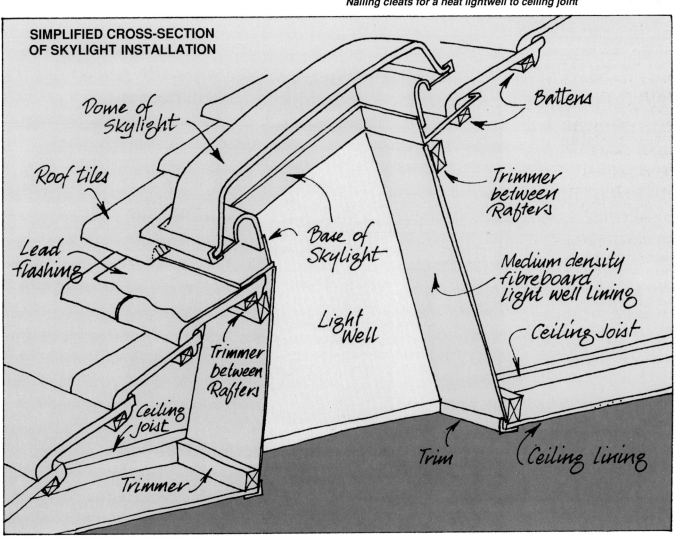

**SIMPLIFIED CROSS-SECTION OF SKYLIGHT INSTALLATION**

Dome of Skylight

Roof tiles

Lead flashing

Base of Skylight

Light Well

Trimmer between Rafters

Ceiling Joist

Trimmer

Battens

Trimmer between Rafters

Medium density fibreboard light well lining

Ceiling Joist

Trim

Ceiling lining

*One of the more noticeable features of modern houses is the way they have been opened up by incorporating a much greater window area. Today, homemakers have a more acute awareness of the great outdoors, a desire for more natural light, and a realisation that correctly designed and placed windows increase the efficiency of winter heating.*

*Project 8*

# More Window
## More natural light

Many people have in fact devalued their home by installing modern windows with very little regard to the period or style of the rest of the building. Larger windows can be made in many different styles and materials. They should be sympathetic and compatible with what is already in place, and are not always a lot more expensive.

This particular project involves the installation of a window in a downstairs brick-veneer wall, that is, one with a timber structural frame, and a veneer of single-skin brickwork on the exterior. A second storey is being supported by the timber frame. The window is a cedar frame with a brand name aluminium sashless horizontal sliding system, using 6 mm thick glass. The size of the window is 950 mm high by 880 mm wide.

**There has been a popular move to upgrade the home by increasing the number and areas of windows facing the sun – to allow winter light and warmth to enter, while keeping the summer sun out. Larger windows may also be desirable to make the most of an outdoor view, whether it is of your garden or a more distant vista.**

*Completed window installation. Note storm mould finishing window to brick joint*

Stegbar and Sydney Window Installation

## WHAT TO BUY

☐ new window, 950 mm high by 880 mm wide, cedar frame with aluminium sashless horizontal sliding operating system with 6 mm thick glass
☐ galvanised steel lintel, 75 mm x 10 mm bar
☐ flashing for top and bottom of window; aluminium core flashing is easiest to mould, and the width should be 300 mm wide. It can always be trimmed if needed

## SPECIAL TOOLS NEEDED

☐ 2 to 4 props
☐ 2 kg club hammer
☐ bolster
☐ plugging chisel
☐ bricklaying tools – shovel, bricklayer's trowel, level

## TIME

One weekend, once you are organised. Any longer and you will have a waterproofing and security problem. Make an early start!

*Timber framing removed and prop support in place*

## STEP BY STEP

*1*  The first step is to decide on the style of window suitable for the house. The new windows should match the existing windows, while providing the amount of extra light required.

*2*  Our window is 880 mm wide and 950 mm high, of cedar construction.

*3*  When you have your window, take the exact outside dimensions, for your mark-out. Our window is 880 mm wide so the opening size will need to be 890 mm horizontally to allow for fitting and squaring. The height of the window is 950 mm, so the opening size should be 960 mm to 970 mm on the inside. This should be the quoted opening size. Allow for the new lintel or window head. On the outside, as well as allowing for the lintel thickness (10 mm), allow for the sill bricks. The sill brick will take a height of about 1.5 bricks. Therefore the exterior opening will be about 1065 mm in height.

*4*  The opening sizes of the window should be roughly marked on the inside. The marking is not critical on the external wall as you will be removing and replacing brickwork to suit the window anyway, and this can be done in relation to the internal timber-frame opening.

*5*  Start by removing the wall lining on the inside to expose the area where the window is to go. It should be removed floor to ceiling, and well past the opening to allow you to work on the frame. Patching smaller strips of linings will be frustrating anyway. You can now see the frame and mark exactly on the frame where the window is to be fitted.

*6*  As the frame is holding up an upper floor and framing, it is important that these joists be supported before you start working. This can be done with the use of a prop for a small opening (in our case) or two if the opening is larger. It is firmly placed on a sole plate of solid timber, and firmly screwed up to a temporary 75 mm x 100 mm timber beam.

*7*  Remove any noggings or

*Timber frame prepared for window, and bricks laid ready to accept window. Note interior prop holding upper floor framing*

39

studs that are in the way, but save them if possible as they will be suitable for the altered framing. Remove all nails. Push any wiring to one side to give a clear working area.

**8** Cut two timber studs to suit. Measure and mark where the bottom of the window head will be on both studs, and make a second mark 50 mm above this. Square lines across the broad face of the stud. Place the studs on your saw stools; saw 5-10 mm depth along each of the four lines, and then chisel out the timber between the cuts. These are called housings. Now fix the two studs either side of the window opening, with the housings facing towards each other, nailing into both head and sole plates. On a small window, single studs would be adequate but if larger openings are required,

secondary 'jack' studs will be needed to support the larger lintel.

**9** Cut and install a sill plate for the bottom of the window. Don't forget to allow for the gaps. Make sure it is installed dead level. Then cut and fix a short jack stud in the centre of the opening under the sill plate.

**10** Across the top, install the head into the housing previously prepared, and install a small packer between the head plate and frame head to complete the inside frame.

**11** Start knocking out bricks on the exterior. If the brickwork is sound, and the joints solid, an opening of 900 mm will most likely be self-supporting. If it does collapse it will be in the form of a triangle of full

*In large openings an angle lintel is used to take the weight over the greater span*

unsupported bricks. Where joints are weak, a 'needle' is needed about halfway between the extremities of the window, and above where the top of the lintel will be. Needles are made of at least 100 mm x 125 mm timber and held both inside and out by props. Once supported the rest of the brickwork can be removed safely.

**12** Bricks are knocked out using a club hammer and bolster. Work from the top and centre of the window opening to the outside edge, and leave a saw-tooth arrangement of bricks, wider than the window, to allow the neat finishing of brickwork to the window edge.

**13** Remove the bottom 38 mm of vertical joints

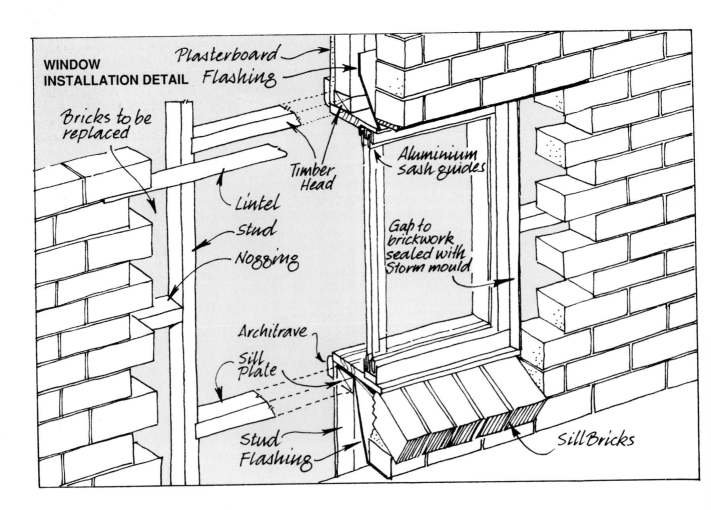

**WINDOW INSTALLATION DETAIL**

Plasterboard
Flashing
Bricks to be replaced
Timber Head
Lintel
stud
Nogging
Aluminium sash guides
Gap to brickwork sealed with Storm mould
Architrave
Sill Plate
Stud Flashing
Sill Bricks

(perpends) between the bricks over where the lintel is to go with a plugging chisel. These act as weep holes for the top flashing.

**14** Once the first full row at the top of the opening is exposed, the top flashing from the timber frame over the top of the lintel can be installed, prior to the lintel being put in place. Fix the flashing 150 mm above the top of the window to studs or lintel if high enough.

**15** The steel lintel can now be put in place and is a further protection against brickwork collapse. Be careful that the flashing is not damaged or caught up. It must have a bearing of about 150 mm both sides.

**16** If necessary, the lintel can be further supported halfway along its length by a prop at a slight angle.

**17** The wall can now be bricked up to the exact outside dimensions of the window opening, finishing with a plumb neat finish to both sides of the opening, and within one horizontal course of bricks to the underside of the sill. The sill bricks are installed later.

**18** It's now time to fit the bottom flashing to the window, if one is not already provided. This runs under the window sill and turns up inside about 12 mm, and on the outside is wide enough in one piece to preferably lap into the mortar joint one brick course below the sill. It should be slightly wider at the sides so that it can be turned up at the edges. In our case, the flashing was installed directly under the sill bricks.

**19** Fit the window in the opening and check for fit. You should have about 5 mm space to either side of the window for packing and adjustment. Make sure the flashing is not caught up.

*Flashing and first sill brick in place. Storm moulding is added after sill bricks*

**20** Check that the window sitting on the sill framing is truly horizontal. Align it so that the internal edge of the window frame overhangs sufficiently to cover the lining, which in most cases is 10 mm. This allows a good finish for the architraves. Some joiners take a slight angled shaving off the outside edge of the reveal to provide a tighter fit for the architrave.

**21** Now check that the vertical is plumb, and use packing between the house frame and the window frame for any adjustments. Pack the other side as well. The packing shouldn't be too tight as you may bend the frame out of shape and the window will bind.

**22** Make sure the window is not twisted, otherwise the sashes won't operate correctly. Then nail in place to the timber frame using galvanised nails to hold everything in place.

**23** Dress the flashings into place. Now install the sill bricks on a drier mortar bed to get the fall with the flashing in place under the sill bricks. The bricks must be cut with the bolster and hammer, and are fitted to within about 10 mm from the underside of the timber. Regardless of where the flashings are, if water is trapped it has to be able to flow out of the cavity. Allow for weep holes to the underside of the sill mortar joints so that water can flow out from the flashing.

**24** Seal the gap between brickwork and timber window with non-hardening mastic.

**25** Replace linings to the inside, and fill and sand all joints as described in the plasterboard section (see Project 4).

**26** Fix architraves for a professional finish.

*Fabric, pelmets and blinds*
*Dressed windows, in the form of curtains, elaborate drapes and blinds, are probably the most decorative type of fabric use in the home. Large or small areas of attractively used fabric can quickly transform a room – so look upon window dressing as interior decorating, as well as a practical essential.*

*Project 9*

# Window Dressing
## Three projects in one

## FABRIC

*Don't have high expectations of fabrics that were never intended for anything other than their specific purpose. So very often a fabric is chosen on the emotional basis of 'I just have to have it!'*

Fabric should first of all be chosen for weight, weave and, sensibly, cost. Then isolate the colours, pattern and texture or sheen that appeals most to you. Generally, the more the fabric will be handled or sat on, the sturdier it has to be. No sensible person would upholster the family room sofa in a lightweight chintz, because chintz is not hard-wearing, has a processed wax surface which does not take kindly to soiling, and creases quite easily! Having said that, chintz is one of the most universally appealing fabrics. It is usually beautifully coloured or designed, with

*Classic swags and tails work well with tall windows and ceilings, and can be ideal positioned over the top of French windows*

great lustre and presence – when used suitably in curtains, bedspreads and cushions it is simply wonderful. In the same way, don't use a heavy linen for your sheer bedroom curtains, or attempt to sew it into loose covers on your lightweight home sewing machine. It's a beautiful and enduring fabric, but is also heavy and sometimes difficult to handle expertly. You will find many different combinations of man-made fibres in fabrics today, and a wonderful assortment of weights of natural fabrics – mostly linen, cotton and, to a large extent, wool for upholstery. Both types have benefits, so be guided by the manufacturer's instructions, your colour preferences and your budget. So, in brief, fabrics have definite purposes, and to ask more of a fabric than is sensible can become a big problem – both financially and aesthetically. Seek advice from the trained assistant in your fabric shop, and also observe what fabrics designers favour when decorating.

## FABRIC CALCULATIONS

When calculating the number of metres required, always measure at least twice and take the process slowly and carefully. If possible, get someone else to check your measurements and allowances. Be sure to allow for matching patterns in printed fabrics, and don't be frugal with hems and good-quality lining. Remember, curtains are a focal point in a room and if they delight the eye you'll be happy to live with them until they wear out. If they irritate you for some reason – too short, wrong colour, too skimpy – you'll be constantly reminded of your mistakes!

## FABRIC SHRINKAGE

Most natural fibres will shrink, so be aware of the manufacturer's instructions about cleaning fabrics. All lined items should be dry-cleaned. At best, when washing curtains do them by hand, do not crease unduly or allow to soak for long periods of time. Allow them to hang straight rather than creased over a line.

## TIE BANDS

A tie band is a simple corded tassel, or an elaborate padded and plaited tie band – the widest choice of options is available here to the home decorator. Tie bands are at once practical and visually exciting. They hold curtains back to allow light through, they create a line to open curtains that is decorative and controlled, and allow you to adjust your curtains to be fuller and softer should your decor demand this.

Tie bands are generally straight, or can be slightly curved. A brown paper pattern cut and adjusted for your situation will help you achieve your ideal tie band. Brass hooks can be purchased that screw onto the wall – simply tuck the curtains behind them – or create your own straight pieces of fabric from curtain scraps. Experiment with fabric borders, padded tie bands, fabric with bias binding edges for emphasis, satin ribbons on sheer fabrics, or elaborate tie bands trimmed with luxurious fringing and gimp braids (upholstery braids, usually vertically woven, often using two or three colours).

*1 Strips of padded fabric plaited to make a tie band. Attach small curtain rings at each end to hook*

*2 A purchased tassel and cord used as a tie band*

*3 A stylish brass curtain band – available at curtain shops – screws into the wall. Simply tuck the curtain behind the curved 'arm'*

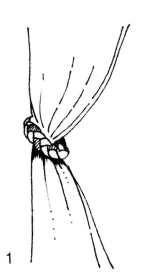

1

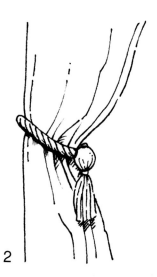

2

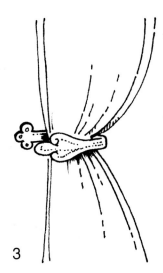

3

# SWAG PELMETS

*Formal swag pelmets are draped pieces of fabric which, when attached to a pelmet support board, become a classic draped pelmet. They hang free of the curtain and usually add a classical, ornate appearance to windows.*

Here are some rules to remember with swag trimmings: they look best on tall windows in rooms with high ceilings, so be sure that you don't over-design your room; consider your fabric requirements (swag curtains can take up large amounts of fabric, and this can become a budget-breaker) – plain calico or home-spun fabric is one idea, as the old principle of using fabric generously applies well here. Generous amounts of inexpensive fabric look wonderful next to skimpy quantities of expensive fabric.

## STEP BY STEP

**Fabric:** The main fabric for the swag is cut on the bias. Allow one-and-a-half times the finished width, which will be the length of the curtain track plus seam allowances, by two-and-a-half times the finished depth, plus hems. Join fabrics as shown, to create a piece large enough, prior to cutting out the swag. It will make your task simpler if you create a paper pattern of your swag shape. Working on a large, flat surface, cut out the lining first, then use this piece as a template to cut the main fabric piece. With right sides facing, stitch lining piece and main piece together around curved edge only.

Clip seam, turn to right side, press. Pin lining and main fabric pieces together around remaining edges, stitch to secure, neatening edges as you go.

Cut a piece of fabric, probably from scraps, that measures the finished width of the swag, plus seam allowances. Mark the centre, and the finished width. Allowing the straight piece of fabric to lie close to the edge of your worktable, secure it to the table surface. Match 'C' of swag to centre of secured fabric, allowing swag piece to hang over edge of table. Working upwards from 'A', fold in rough pleats until you reach 'B'. Adjust these folds or pleats until you are satisfied with the way they lie and their evenness. Repeat for the other side, pleating from 'E' up to 'D'. When you are satisfied with the lie of the pleats and that the width of the swag matches your straight fabric strip, pin and stitch the pleats to the fabric strip. Trim this fabric strip back to 3 cm in depth.

It is important to estimate fabric quantities accurately; to cut the fabric correctly; and to observe bias cut sections, as these need to fall and drape in deep folds.

**Swags:** Swags need to be in proportion to the completed length of your curtains. As a guide to depths of finished swags, reckon on the swag finishing at one sixth to one eighth of the window height.

**Tails with even vertical folds:** Tails are generally a third to one-half the height of the window but, again, proportion is important and you are the best judge of what suits your particular window size. The length of the short inner vertical edge is again up to you but a third to one-half of the outside length is a good starting point.

The width of the finished tail can be estimated by pleating brown paper to approximate the desired size. Use this measurement as the width of the top edge of the tails. Your template should look like a triangle with the inner top corner cut away. When purchasing lining fabric, remember that it will be seen when the tail is pleated. The colour and texture of the lining is important, and can become an added decorative note. Cut out lining piece, then, using this shape as a pattern, cut main fabric piece.

With right sides facing, stitch lining and main fabric tail pieces together, leaving top edge open. Trim corners, clip seams for ease and turn to right side. Press. Following the instructions for pleating the swag, cut a scrap of fabric the finished width of the pleated tail, plus seam allowances. Pleat tail into this width and, when satisfied with lie and evenness, stitch to scrap strip. Trim scrap strip to 3 cm depth. Repeat for matching tail or tails.

**Support Board:** The most secure way to affix swags and tails is to a support board cut to the width of the curtain track, and to a depth that

## SWAG PATTERN

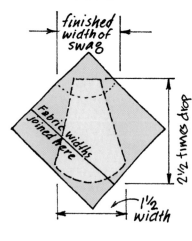

*How to plan and measure your swag pattern*

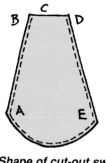

*Shape of cut-out swag*

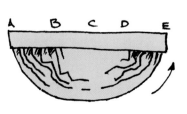

*Completed swag with strip of fabric applied ready for attachment to support board*

**Pleating the sides of the swag**

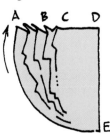

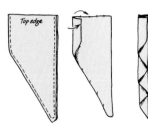

*Pattern and how to pleat tails*

allows the swag and tails to hang free of the curtains. Cover the board with fabric, secured with tacks, glue or staples, and secure the board to the wall with L-shaped brackets at either end. Tack the top tails and then the top of the swag into place along the top of this board.

**Fixing to the support board:** First you must bind the edges of the swag and tails with a flap of fabric that finishes at the same depth as the support board. Cut fabric pieces the length of the finished swag and tails plus seam allowances; with right sides facing, stitch one long side of binding strip to swag and each tail piece.

Press 1 cm to wrong side of remaining long side. Fold binding strip to have right sides facing, stitch short ends, fold binding strip to its right side. Press. Hand or machine stitch to previous row of stitching. You now have a flap that is the length and depth of the support board.

*Gentle colours coordinating in matched fabrics bring a restful feeling to a bedroom. The tailored pelmet and tie-backs are trimmed with matching braid*

# TAILORED PELMETS

*These decorative elements have outgrown their stuffy and slightly old-fashioned image of the past. They can now, with clever choices and use of fabric, totally complement what is really a plain set of curtains, and transform a room into a well-thought-out home decorator's triumph.*

Some are shaped, others are simple gathered valances or short frills matching the curtains. Others are padded, and some are swags of matching fabric. There are many options available, and most are easy for the home decorator to achieve. Most pelmets depend on a support board being fixed to the wall either side of the curtains. Be sure that you allow sufficient room for the curtains to bunch together when open.

Simple trimmed padded pelmets are a tailored trim for simple pleated curtains. You will need a support board as described in the Step by Step for Swag Pelmets – again, long enough to allow the pelmet to hang free of the curtain at the front and at the side return area.

Fix this to the wall with L-shaped brackets. Be sure to allow space for the curtains to bunch up when open, and do not position the brackets so as to interfere with this bunching.

In general, pelmets are of the same fabric as the curtains, often with complementary braid trimming. They are stiffened with interfacing, and lined.

## STEP BY STEP

Generally pelmet depth is one-eighth of the overall drop of the curtains, plus about 20 cm for hems and upper turnover allowances. Width is the length of the support board plus the distance from the front of the support board to the wall, plus seam allowances.

Decide how you wish the pattern in your fabric to run,

and cut and join pieces to achieve this if necessary. Cut out a lining piece the same size as the main fabric piece.

Iron on interfacing to the back of the main fabric piece. With right sides facing and raw edges matching, stitch around all edges of main pelmet piece and lining, leaving a small opening for turning. Turn, press. Stitch one row of Velcro to the top side of the pelmet by hand, or by machine if corresponding trim on the right side of the pelmet conceals this stitching. Trim front of pelmet if desired. Glue or staple opposite Velcro strip to front and side edges of support board. Secure pelmet to edge of board by pressing Velcro bands together.

45

# BEAUTIFUL BLINDS

*Blinds have travelled a long way from their origins as the gauze window protectors of elaborate drapes and furnishings in grand houses. Modern blinds can be totally functional and unobtrusive, or unashamedly ornate and extravagant.*

## ROMAN BLINDS

These blinds are tailored and neat looking, economical in their use of fabric and regarded as being quite simple to make. There is less sewing in this style of blind than, say, a festoon blind, and they lend themselves to stripes or evenly printed geometric fabrics very well.

### STEP BY STEP

The blind is traditionally fitted inside the window frame, and has a series of cords that are pulled or released to raise and lower the blind. These cords are held together and are wound around a metal cleat that has been fastened to the window frame. The best cord is a fine nylon cord that is flexible and not more than 6-8 mm thick.

The cord runs through a series of metal cording rings screwed into the back of timber support laths that are inserted through sewn tucks in the blind (see our illustration for the positions of these elements). To line or not to line – this is the question! Some fabrics simply have to be lined, especially those with strong patterns, or those blinds that have to block out most of the light. Interfacing is ironed on to the back of the main fabric piece and this in itself will block out most of the light, and, providing your hems are neat and evenly stitched, may be all you need.

Should you decide that lining is the only way for you to go, cut your lining piece 5 cm smaller all round than your main blind piece. Position the lining on the wrong side of the main piece, fold in your 5 cm-deep hems, stitch, then treat this piece as one layer of fabric. Fabric requirements will depend on how many pleats you desire, and the depth of the timber laths you use. The basic size of the blind is calculated thus: The width of the window frame (inner or wherever you wish the blind to sit) plus the depth. Add 5 cm hems to the sides and lower edge, plus 30 cm in length for folding over the top timber support lath. Add to this figure approximately 12 cm for each lath pocket you decide to have. The best way to calculate their distance apart is to divide the length of the window into sixths or eighths, allowing room at the very top of the blind for the folds to bunch when the blind is pulled up.

Again, the easiest way to calculate all this is to make a pattern of the blind from brown paper, creasing in the folds, hems and the area folded over the top support lath. It is easy to re-crease the paper until you are satisfied with the spacing and length. Remember that, ideally, when the blind is fully down it should lie flat – with no remaining folds.

## AUSTRIAN BLINDS

These blinds are delightfully stylish, can look dramatic or feminine, and are remarkably easy to make. They usually work well on their own, but can be complemented by side drapes that are not pulled closed. Austrian blinds can be made in sheer fabric, and indeed, this is their ideal weight of fabric, as they originally were intended to allow light through, but to give some sense of privacy to the room. These blinds are permanently ruched from top to base in vertical rows, creating crescents of curved fabric, held in place by integral rows of cording rings on the reverse side. They pull up and are released by fine cording threaded through these rings.

## ROLLER BLINDS

Roller blinds are a traditional, simple form of window trimming that can be made at home. They are backed with a firm, iron-on interfacing or bonding fabric and usually have some form of trimming at the lower edge. They are fixed to a support lath or roller, and are secured to brackets set into the window frame. They are most suitable where light has to be eliminated; where decorative details are not demanded and simplicity is the key; and where space for curtains is not available. Often they fit behind curtains most unobtrusively, as they roll up neatly and do not create bulk.

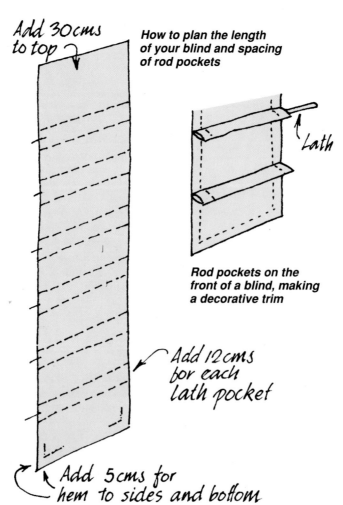

Add 30 cms to top

**How to plan the length of your blind and spacing of rod pockets**

Lath

**Rod pockets on the front of a blind, making a decorative trim**

Add 12 cms for each lath pocket

Add 5 cms for hem to sides and bottom

*A classic roman blind leaves the area around a window free of clutter. These blinds are ideal for tailored or masculine rooms, and can show off bold-patterned fabric beautifully*

*There is nothing quite like a well-designed and well-made leadlight window. Pinpoints of light and flashes of colour can transform a boring window with a poor view, into a major feature. Leadlighting is one of those projects that should not perhaps be undertaken as a one-off project.*

# Lovely Leadlights
## Enhancing your view

**Top:** *Entrance showing front door with leadlight panels, and leadlight porthole*
**Left:** *Detail of porthole*

The equipment necessary to get started on your own leadlight project involves considerable expense – but the materials that you buy will provide lots of bits and pieces for later projects.

In the case of this kitchen, new leadlight was installed to obscure the view – a neighbour's rooftop. The new leadlight was carefully made to match the existing leadlight

Hallway fan lights as leadlight panels

Leadlight for landing

*Leadlighting is an art as much as a trade. The effectiveness of the window depends on the design and colour section as much as workmanship. If you are keen to learn how to leadlight, consider joining a leadlighting class, where equipment and materials will be available for a reasonable cost.*

*Project 10*

# Leadlight Porthole

## STEP BY STEP

*NOTE:* When working with lead make sure that you clean your hands before breaking for meals. Washing hands thoroughly after leaving the workshop should be automatic as lead is an accumulative poison.

*1* Set up an area to work in that is flat and will not damage the glass. A workbench with a chipboard top is ideal. A felt covering will prevent scratching to the glass. As work progresses the surface should be frequently vacuumed of glass splinters as these may damage or break glass being cut.

*2* Finalise your design. This is often the slowest part of the job, but many books on the subject have a number of designs that can be used or adapted. Try to avoid designs where tight curves or sharp internal corners need to be cut, because you probably won't be successful. Plain shapes with relatively simple curves are easiest to cut and lead up.

*3* Once the miniature design is finished, make several copies and colour them in with the colours you've selected. It may be worthwhile trying several combinations of colours to get the leadlight just right.

**The project featured is not the easiest leadlighting project to start off with, but will give an indication of what is achievable in this medium. There is a wide lead edge, and three sizes of thin lead for effect.**

Hold them in place in the position they are to go, in a variety of light conditions.

*4* Measure the window. In this case, it is a 415 mm circular window. Deduct half the width of the lead (came) in this case about 7 mm, plus additional 3 mm from the circle all round to allow for fitting. Large 'H' section lead is used on edges to allow for trimming should the pattern slightly 'grow' while being made. Therefore the pattern (cartoon) size is finalised at 400 mm in diameter.

*5* Transfer your design to the full pattern size and make a full-scale drawing of the window. Do it in pencil first to ensure it is right. Then finally draw it in heavy felt pen to leave a line about 1.5 mm thick between the glass pieces. This automatically makes an allowance for the wall thickness of the lead section.

*6* Make a couple of copies of the pattern, so that they can be used for numbering glass pieces, or cut into individual pieces and used as templates for cutting the glass (if you find that easiest), or if one gets damaged or torn.

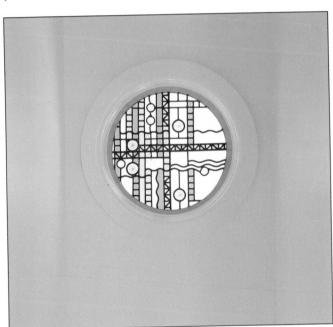

*The completed project in place*

*7* Mount your main cartoon on a piece of particleboard (chipboard) or similar, with plenty of room to work around the edges of the design. Normally , two battens are fixed to the board against which you can work. In the case of this circular design, mark out and cut a panel to fit against the battens, and mark out and cut a semi circle to hold the lead in place. In this example, glass was used as the panel, but you can use thin plywood as well.

*8* Choose the glass for each shape according to the colours worked out; buy it and have it ready to start. Similarly, have the lead ready as well as horseshoe nails and all other needs.

*9* Cut the first piece of glass to size. This should be a piece of scrap just for practice. Start the cut a small distance in from the edge of the glass. Apply steady pressure without stopping, and hold the cutter close to 90°. Draw it towards you, and let it roll over the

**10** To break the glass, hold it vertically and place your two index fingers under either side of the cut, and your thumbs on top of the glass – the knuckles should be touching. Rotate both hands down, or clockwise and anticlockwise, and the glass should break and 'run' along your score line. Shake off any glass splinters.

**11** If the glass will not break itself, lightly tap under the score line with the hammer on the non-cutting end of the glass cutter. Hold the glass close to the score line to avoid breakage.

**12** If you are still unsuccessful using fingers, you may have to invest in a pair of 'cut running pliers', to do the job. When cutting thin strips it may be necessary to use grozing pliers to grip the narrow side, or you may injure your hand if you slip. Glass cut in this way will never be as neat as when it is cut by running.

**13** When cutting the glass for actual leadlight, mark out from the cartoon directly, or the cut-out pieces. Cut the large pieces first as the offcuts may then be used for smaller pieces of the same colour. Aim at being economical within reason.

**14** Once cut, hold each piece against your pattern and make sure it fits between the inked-in lines. If it overlaps it will need trimming with the grozing pliers. If it is too small it will need to be recut.

**15** Generally leadlighters like to cut all the glass pieces to shape before starting the leading. The pieces can be laid on the spare cartoon, or each piece can be numbered on the face side with a corresponding number on the spare cartoon. The pieces can be carefully laid in a box until ready for use.

**16** Before lead can be used it must be stretched, and this is done with a lead vice and pliers. This must be done with care so that when applying pressure the lead does not snap and you end up on the floor. Once stretched, the channels of the lead may need to be opened using a lathekin.In some areas you may be able to purchase pre-stretched lead.

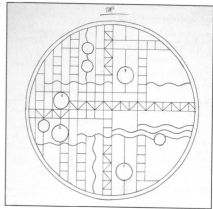

**Template of leadlight porthole**

**Drawing of porthole showing different colour sections of leadlight**

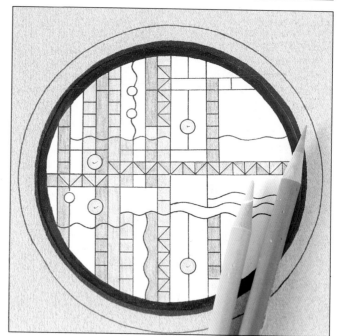

*17* Cut off the two damaged ends of the lead, and then cut sufficient length off the wider lead to place around the semi circle defined by the cut panel. The lead is cut using a sharp lead knife, in a rocking motion. The other half of the perimeter is the last piece in the jigsaw to be fitted at the end.

*18* Select the piece of glass for the starting point. On our circle it can just about be anywhere on the bottom perimeter, but where successive pieces can be installed easily. The best place would be in the middle.

*19* This particular window was made by building up from the bottom filling in all the lower area, and then working up the centre and out to the sides, one at a time.

*20* Insert the first piece of glass, gently tapping it into place with the wooden end of the lead knife, and hold it in place with horseshoe nails,

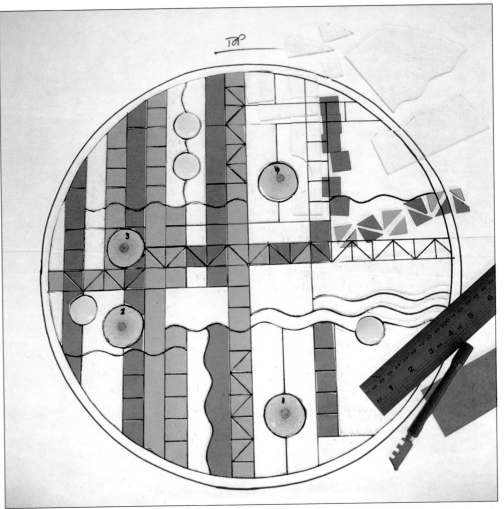

**Cut glass for leadlight porthole**

flat side of nails against the glass. Cut a length of the internal (thinner) lead slightly longer than the edge to be joined, and insert the adjoining glass into the lead. Hold in place using the horseshoe nails again. Mark the joint of the two glass pieces on the lead, getting the angle right, and remove the lead. Make another mark just back from this first one, and cut the lead slightly short. This allows for the next lead, which crosses the first one, to sit properly with an accurate joint that will be easy to solder. Slowly continue in this fashion, fanning out across the window, building up the leadlight.

*21* Always hold each new piece or section with the

horseshoe nails. Never use the nails against the lead as they will cause irreparable damage with the lead being so soft. When the entire light has been made, the final outside wider came is fitted in place. You are ready for soldering the joints. Measure the panel for size and square the corners if applicable.

*22* Just before soldering, ensure that no flanges from the lead are bent onto the glass or out of shape, because once soldered they will be set.

*23* Soldering is done with an 80 watt iron, as this heats up quickly. Lower wattage irons can be used, but may be a little slower. The easiest tip to use is a 'hook nose' tip, or angled tip as shown opposite.

The tip should be properly tinned before use. Soldering must be carried out in the presence of flux, which removes oxide from the surface of the lead, and provides a good surface for the solder to adhere to. Solid flux is easiest to clean up afterwards, so is recommended. Rub the flux over the joint to be soldered.

*24* Start soldering at the furthest point away from where you are standing. Hold the iron close to the lead, and take a small blob of solder from the stick. Place this on the joint. This should run onto the joint, and when the iron is removed will soon set. Use a little at a time, you can always add more if the joint looks scantly soldered.

**25** When all the joints are soldered, take a wire brush and brush off all traces of flux on the window. Any solder spilt on the glass or lead should peel off as well.

**26** Turn the window over, together with the base as the window is still not strong. Repeat the soldering on the back side. Once again, remove the leftover flux.

**27** It's now time to putty the window. It must be done in one sitting, as otherwise it will set and leave oil stains. Use pre-prepared leadlighting cement, which has been made with carbon black. Wear old clothes as this is a messy job. Force the cement under the lead flanges with whatever you find easiest, thumbs or the lathekin. Do not press down too hard on the glass as the panels can break very easily. Excess cement can be removed by carefully scraping with the lathekin or by using a horseshoe nail alongside the lead. The cement will come away.

**28** At this stage sprinkle whiting over the surface of the whole window and scrub vigorously to clean the window. Don't press too hard, as the whole window is still a little soft and may distort. Repeat the process on the other side.

**29** Let the window stand, rather than lie, for a few days to allow the cement to harden. After three or so days, decide whether you would like a grey or black finish. If grey, simply polish the window with a bristle brush. If you want the lead to be black, apply some well-mixed stove black with a brush. After a few minutes, when the solvent has evaporated, polish with a brush once again. Now install the window in the frame prepared.

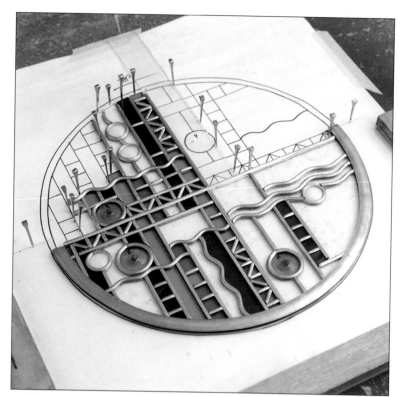

*Assembling the glass pieces and lead, filling design from bottom*

**Soldering lead joints with 'hook nose' soldering iron**

*Choosing the right floor and floorcovering is an important aspect of furnishing your home – it is not only one of the most dominant decorative surfaces, it will also claim a large proportion of your furnishing budget.*

# THE PERFECT FLOOR

## An important aspect of furnishing your home

The type and quality of the floorcovering you choose should be appropriate for each room, just as the right colour and design are important. Poor quality flooring, ill-suited to the requirements of the room, will wear out quickly and end up costing you a lot more in the long run.

**Cork floor for kitchen/dining area**

### FLOOR CONSTRUCTION MATERIALS

**Concrete:** An artificial rock which is normally on the ground in homes, but in certain instances may be suspended. 'Slab on ground' refers to concrete laid on a membrane directly onto prepared foundation soil. Raft slabs are designed to float on poor foundation soils. Good drainage is essential. A suspended concrete floor refers to concrete supported off the ground on a base structure. Concrete is rigid and offers good thermal mass and soundproofing.

**Timber:** This is still the most commonly used material for domestic floors built on honeycomb walls. It may be a strip floor of individual solid timber boards, or a sheet material such as chipboard or plywood. Timber provides a more resilient floor, but must be properly ventilated underneath to prevent moisture and rot problems. Tempered chipboard is resistant to

moisture and therefore especially suitable for wet areas.

**Brick:** Mainly used in the province of alternative builders; also used as paving.

### UNDERLAYS

Many flooring finishes are not fixed directly to the main structural floor but to an underlay to ensure that the type of floor has no effect on the final finish. Common materials used as underlays are plywood for rigid and resilient tiles, hardboard for resilient tiles, and various applied materials, usually where rigid floor finishes are applied to non-rigid floor structures. Floor levelling compounds are also available.

### FLOOR FINISHES

**Coatings:** Timber structural floors can be sanded and finished with clear finishes, but other structural floor materials are normally covered.

**Resilient tiles:** These include studded rubber, vinyl in many variations, cork and cork composite,

*Dining/family room with herringbone pattern block parquetry floor*

*Terracotta and ceramic tiles. Note the correct grout joints*

and linoleum. They are available in many colours and easy to keep looking good.

**Sheet materials:** These include sheet vinyls and linoleum, otherwise similar to tiles.

**Parquetry:** Consists of small timber strips or blocks, laid in various patterns, adhered to the floor and then clear finished. They are also now available in loose-lay interlocking tiles. Parquetry must be kept dry, or it will buckle.

**Ceramic and quarry tiles:** Now popular in most rooms of the house. The choice is from among ceramic, monocottura (single-fired), extruded quarry and terracotta tiles, available in various glaze levels and as non-slip tiles. They must be isolated from movement by slip joints or flexible

adhesives, and have allowances made for expansion and contraction.

**Stone:** Most commonly used are slate and quartzite. More prestige materials increasing in popularity are marble, travertine and granite. They are all rigid and require a rigid subfloor.

**Carpet:** Commonplace in most homes. Now choices include not only woven styles and patterns, but also materials such as wools, nylons, acrylics and other man-made fibres, as well as blends for all applications. It is important to match the expected traffic of the carpet to the carpet's classification.

*Light vinyl floor with dark accent tiles*

*Polished hardwood timber-strip floor*

*Sanding and sealing your timber floor*
*One of the simplest and most attractive floors is the polished timber-strip floor. In many a renovation or restoration, old floors of hard-to-get and well-seasoned timbers can be exposed, and brought to light in all their original glory by careful sanding and clear finishing.*

*Project 11*

# Timber-strip Floor

This project involves sanding and sealing a timber-strip floor. Sanding floors properly is not easy and the equipment used is heavy and powerful, requiring a certain amount of strength to operate efficiently. There will be occasions, especially with problem floors, when even the most diehard do-it-yourselfer should seek professional help and advice.

**For a new room, or when replacing a floor, there is nothing quite like a timber-strip floor. It's not an easy project, but is well worth the effort – even if you hire a professional to do it.**

## STEP BY STEP

*1* The first step is to decide whether or not the floor is worth doing; if it is badly damaged it will never look good. This investigation should also include checking under the floor to ensure that there is adequate ventilation. If the ventilation is poor, the floor will need improvement before work on the surface begins.

*2* The floor should be cordonned off from the time work starts to stop any possible staining, dirt or other contaminants affecting the floor.

*3* Any tacks from old carpet should be removed. Any old accumulations of adhesive

*Finished timber-strip floor. Detail: Applying coating on timber using a lamb's wool pad*

## WHAT TO BUY
- ☐ polyurethane finish
- ☐ 1 litre solvent

## SPECIAL TOOLS NEEDED
- ☐ nail punch (3 mm)
- ☐ drum sander (hire)
- ☐ disc sander (designed for flooring; also hired)
- ☐ lamb's wool pad and long-handled extension
- ☐ 50 mm or 75 mm brush
- ☐ face mask and cartridge suitable for hydrocarbons
- ☐ hand-sanding float

## TIME
Two weekends, on and off. The final sanding and first coating should be on the same day to protect the newly sanded surface from accidental staining.

should be scraped off as far as possible.

**4** All nails should be punched to about 3 mm below the surface.

**5** Sanding can now commence. The procedure will depend on the state of the floor. The sander should initially be fitted with a coarse grade abrasive, about #40 grade. This will level and cut into the floor. Normally three passes are made across the floor. The first at 45° to the direction of the floorboards. At no time should the machine be stationary while the drum is revolving as this will cause a 'stop mark' or depression on the floor.

**6** The second pass is at right angles to the first.

**7** Clean the floor and vacuum, especially around the nail holes. Any splits, small depressions and nail holes should be stopped (filled) at this stage with a good-quality wood filler. Fill the holes well.

**8** When the cleaning and filling work is dry, the final cut with the coarse abrasive can be carried out parallel to the floorboards.

**9** The areas close to the walls or skirtings that cannot be reached by the drum sander need to be sanded carefully with the disc sander. Progress should be slow and careful as swirl marks are easily made. Any inaccessible areas will have to be scraped level or planed by hand.

**10** The sanding belt now needs to be replaced with one of #80 to #120 grade, and the same three passes are made to remove all scratch marks. This should leave a smooth surface suitable for coating. Once again, the edges need to be carefully sanded with the disc sander, using #120 to #150 grade abrasive. Check for nails before sanding with fine papers. On completion sweep up the dust and vacuum thoroughly.

**11** Apply the first coat of sealer once the sanded area has been cleaned. Brush around the perimeter, and follow this by using a lamb's wool pad to apply the finish

over the broad floor areas. This is made easier if the pad is on an extension handle. When the surface is dry, lightly sand it by hand using a float. An alternative is a short-to-medium nap roller.

**12** Apply a second coat, allow it to dry and then sand it again. The final coat must be carefully applied. Shut all windows and doors to ensure that no dust or wind-blown matter can land and settle on the finish coat.

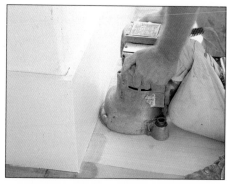

*Sanding edges with a disc sander*
*Below: Sanding machine on final pass*

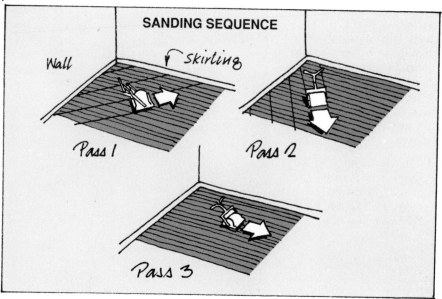

SANDING SEQUENCE

Wall — Skirting

Pass 1

Pass 2

Pass 3

*Slate floor for a family room*
*Slate has enjoyed great popularity with home improvers for many years, because of its toughness and range of natural earthy colours, which can vary from soft green to deep purple, mottled brown and dark charcoal.*

*Project 12*

# Slate Floor

The choice of slate is usually made against other hard floorcoverings such as quarry or monocottura (single-fired) tiles, ceramic floor tiles, and other natural stones such as quartzite, marble, sandstone or granite. Slate is unique in that it is naturally a highly laminated rock and the working of this material differs in some ways to most of the other tiling materials.

Slates are available in a range of sizes, colours and durabilities and are highly regarded for their heat retention properties in passive solar houses.

The colouring of slates is due to the mineral content, and is essentially non-fading. The multicoloured slates are also coloured by weathering along the lamination planes – this may wear off over time in heavy traffic areas unless protected.

Most multicoloured slates are available in sawn edge. These have a neater appearance than the guillotine-edge style.

**The project is to apply slate to a family room, where its lasting strength will provide good service. We have chosen to use attractive 300 mm x 200 mm brown multicoloured slates. The floor at present is a timber-based particleboard (chipboard) floor. The floor area is 5.2 m x 3.6 m. It runs into a kitchen, which will also be done in slate.**

*Dark, multicoloured slate floor in open-plan dining/kitchen/family area*

The Slate People

## WHAT TO BUY

Slate is commonly sold by the square metre (sq.m). To get the area of a room in square metres simply measure the length and width of the room then multiply the measurements.

If the tiles will be bought on a per-piece basis, take the dimensions of each tile and add 6 mm to the dimensions for the joint – then calculate the number required for the whole area. This quantity is for a total area of approximately 19 sq.m, or 320 individual tiles.

- ☐ slates (see above)
- ☐ sufficient hessian and bitumen underlay for the floor area
- ☐ slate-laying adhesive (enough for a cover of 19 sq. m – preferable to cement mortar)

## SPECIAL TOOLS NEEDED

- ☐ string line and pins (or bricks) for setting out
- ☐ straight edge for aligning
- ☐ builder's square, which can be made up in large sizes in timber using the 3:4:5 Pythagoras rule
- ☐ selection of buckets for dry-mix and fully prepared adhesive
- ☐ hammer, wooden-handled, for help in bedding tiles
- ☐ sponge and scouring pads for cleaning of work
- ☐ trowel for spreading adhesive, usually with 12 mm notches

## STEP BY STEP

**1**  Slate must be laid on a firm base that will support it. Timber floors provide a problem in that timber and particleboard (chipboard) expand during humid periods, and shrink during drier times. Timber floors can be prepared in several ways. Care should be taken with all the procedures however, bearing in mind that timber or particleboard (chipboard) are not the best base materials for slate.

**2**  A number of slate suppliers have specially developed membrane systems available for the installation of slate on a timber floor. The one used here is the hessian and bitumen method and will provide the necessary 'slip' joint between the rigid tiles and the timber.

**3**  Clean the floor thoroughly, and punch any protruding nails below the surface.

**4**  Tack the hessian to the floor and apply the bitumen material to the rate specified by the manufacturer. Ensure it is well worked through the hessian, and achieves good contact with the floor. The hessian acts as reinforcement in the bitumen.

**5**  Allow this to dry overnight.

**6**  Now the tiling can be laid out. As slates are more difficult to trim than normal tiles, we have laid them against two walls that are at right angles (checked using the 3:4:5 rule). Dry-lay a row of tiles along the two walls. Ensure that the cuts required at the ends of the row are greater than 50 mm, as smaller cuts result in very brittle pieces of slate that are difficult to bed. The rest of the room can then be squared from these rows. Also remember that slates should not be butted up hard against each other, but should have a 6 mm grouting gap to allow for any thermal movement in either the slate or the surface on which it is laid.

**7**  Slates are not uniform in thickness. It makes the job much easier if they are sorted into similar relative thicknesses before even mixing the mortar. If, for instance, four separate piles were made, each with tiles of a similar thickness, they can be used in rank of thickness, on mortar beds of constant thickness. If you use the thickest tiles first, the mortar bed can gradually be increased for the thinner tiles as the job progresses.

**8**  It may be that some of the slates are slightly bowed. If so, they should be laid with the bow up. If they are laid the other way up it is difficult to provide a strong enough edge-bearing for the tile, and with time it will tend to loosen.

**9**  If you are a first-time slate layer it is probably easier, though more expensive, to use a proprietary adhesive and to follow the instructions closely. Most adhesives are cement based with a fine aggregate, together with workability additives and bonding agents already included. These provide a reasonable working time, so that you have more time to

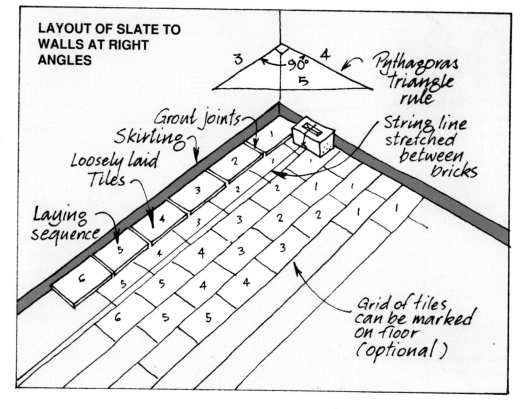

**LAYOUT OF SLATE TO WALLS AT RIGHT ANGLES**

3 — 90° — 4 — 5 — *Pythagoras triangle rule*

*Grout joints*
*Skirting*
*Loosely laid Tiles*
*Laying sequence*
*String line stretched between bricks*
*Grid of tiles can be marked on floor (optional)*

*Underlay hessian and bitumen*

*Laying down of slate in adhesive*

*Grouting the joints*

## TIPSTRIP

### PYTHAGORAS' RULE
Pythagoras' rule states that any triangle where the sides are exactly in the ratio of 3:4:5 will have an exact right angle between the sides of 3 and 4 units. This can be used to advantage to make up large right angles.

### QUARTER IT
In some cases, no walls will be found to be square. In this case, find the centre of the area and establish a cross with a perfect right angle. One of the lines should be parallel with a long wall, and spaced at such a distance that no slates need be cut along that wall. This will divide the room so that you can tile each quarter in turn.

### CARE OF SLATE
Day-to-day care only requires mopping with warm water. Avoid using heavy-duty cleansing agents as these may affect the colour of the slates where the sealer is wearing thin. Resealing should only be necessary every two or three years in all but the heaviest traffic areas. Usually one coat of the same sealer will be sufficient. Bear in mind that glassware dropped on slate will break!

carry out adjustments and take levels. All are water mixable and washable while wet.

**10** Once you are happy with the design and layout, the adhesive can be mixed. Bear in mind that many of the proprietary brand mixtures require you to leave the mix standing for up to 15 minutes before use. Most mixes remain workable for around 2 hours in the summer and 3 hours in the winter. After this period of time the adhesive should be discarded.

**11** Mix enough adhesive for about 1-2 sq.m at a time and finish this amount of tiling before mixing more. This will easily be worked in the time spans available. Spread the adhesive over the area where you intend to start the tiling, and notch it using a 12 mm notched trowel.

**12** Place the tile in the right position and gently rock it into position. The slate should be manoeuvred from the centre, and the gentle back-and-forward rocking should force most of the air out from underneath the tile. The final positioning can be done using the wooden handle of a hammer, tapping the tile only near the centre. It helps if the other hand is placed on the tile, as this provides shock absorption so that the tile doesn't just rock

around its spot and actually loosen the bond.

**13** Every now and again remove a tile that has been properly laid, just to monitor that the bedding is covering the whole of the back of the tile, and that the consistency of the mortar is correct, with minimal air holes.

**14** When you are happy with one tile, proceed to the next.

**15** Once about a metre square of tiles has been laid, it is time to clean off any excess mortar or adhesive, before it sets and stains the tile. This is best done with a damp sponge and frequent changes of water. The sponge should only be damp and must be used gently, otherwise the mortar may be pulled out of the joints, which will stain the slate further. Remove as much as possible with the sponge; the rest can be removed by a scouring pad at the end of a day's work. The aim is not to have to take any remedial action such as acid washing at a later date, as acids can affect the colour of the slate.

**16** The tiles should be left for at least 24 hours before they are grouted.

**17** The grout is usually the same mix as was used for laying. Once again, make sure you clean the tiles thoroughly to prevent

stubborn stains.

**18** Once you have grouted the tiles, allow a further 24 hours to pass before walking on the tiled area.

**19** Slates are normally sealed on interior surfaces. Premature sealing, or sealing while there is any moisture in the slate or in the mortar, may lead to a milky stain forming. This is a white soluble salt that can badly stain the tiles as it forms when water evaporates from the surface. All evaporation must have stopped before you begin sealing or the moisture and any salt will be trapped. At worst, the salt can effect a slow break-down in the entire slate finish.

**20** Sealing is done with either an acrylic or polyurethane coating system. Acrylic is easier as it is water based. It is not advisable to use any products other than those specifically designed for use on slates. Our coloured slates rely in part on the colour of the weathering bands, and should be thoroughly brushed to remove any excess powder, which could cause the sealer to fail. Application can be carried out by sponge. Refer to the directions on the manufacturer's container when recoating or for any other special requirements.

*One of the most successful types of floorcovering for a kitchen is cork tiling. The colour of cork is fairly neutral and these days can be natural, stained, or dyed to various colours. The finish applied is easy to care for, and the job can be done by any handyperson.*

*Project 13*

# Cork Floor

**Our project kitchen and family room is a large area, just under 50 sq. m. The original floor is structural plywood. There are three steps between the kitchen and family areas, which will be edged with light-coloured seasoned hardwood as a wearing edge.**

Cork is available in 4.5 mm or 6 mm thickness. For a kitchen or any heavy-traffic area, the thicker cork should be used. Cork is also available pre-finished or natural. Natural cork has to be completely coated when laid on the floor. This is preferable as the coating will form a seamless finish which is highly resistant to penetration by liquids.

*Finished cork floor with steps to kitchen area*

## STEP BY STEP

### FAMILY ROOM

*1* A timber floor to be covered in cork must be well ventilated. The surface coating acts as a vapour barrier upwards, and moisture in the floor or subfloor will cause failure of the floor or premature rot to the underside.

*2* Check the floor for level. Any undulations should be sanded out, or in very bad cases a floor-levelling compound could be used.

*3* Make sure all nails are well nailed down. There should be no protruding heads.

*4* If skirting is not already there, and is wanted, install it securely to the wall.

*5* The floor should be sanded to ensure there are no local projections or loose areas. This can be done by a professional sanding company, or with care you could do it yourself. (See Project 11 on sanding a timber-strip floor.)

*6* Sweep the floor, then thoroughly vacuum it to ensure that no foreign matter or dust remains.

*7* Bring all the underlay into the room and, if packaged up, open and stand or lay the hardboard underlay around the room for at least 24 hours to acclimatise the underlay to the room. Make sure that air can circulate freely around the sheets.

*8* Fix a hardwood or similar edge nosing to the tread edge of the steps. It must be rebated to allow for depth of underlay, plus the thickness of the cork. It could be milled to shape by your local timber merchant. If you have access to a saw bench or router the strips could be prepared at home. Glue and nail the strips in place.

*9* Lay out the underlay, smooth side up, across the existing flooring. The sheets should not run in the same direction as the grain of the floor. It is also important to stagger the joints, and not to allow any joints in the hardboard to coincide with joints in the flooring. Leave half-millimetre joints between the sheets.

**10** Apply a panel adhesive from a cartridge gun following the manufacturer's recommendations, to ensure that there is no drumminess or movement between the timber floor and the underlay.

**11** Fix the hardboard with special underlay nails. This is a tedious job, as each sheet should be fixed every 75 mm around its perimeter, and at 150 mm centres over the rest of the sheet. This means you will use 91 nails per sheet. Ensure the nails are driven to just beneath the surface. An alternative would be to hire a nail gun, and to use staples to fix the sheets. This is a lot easier on the hands.

**12** Apply strips of hardboard to the tread surfaces of the steps. The risers of the steps do not need an underlay.

**13** Sand all the joints in the hardboard smooth and, again, ensure that all nails are below the surface. Depending on the adhesive used for the cork, the sanded areas may need to be sealed first.

**14** Thoroughly vacuum the floor.

**15** Mark out the floor. It is normal to divide it into quarters, roughly in the centre. To find the centre of the room, mark in two lines each drawn between the centre points of opposite walls. The easiest way to do this is to use a chalkline. Stretch it between the walls, and give the line a flick. The chalk will mark the exact line you need. Where they cross is the centre.

**16** The angle at which they cross should be checked to ensure that it is a right angle. You may have a builder's square, or you could use the Pythagoras 3:4:5 rule to ensure a right angle.

**17** Next dry-lay a row of cork tiles to the skirting wall to see how they work out when they reach the wall. Adjust the starting point to allow a small cut from the edge of the perimeter tiles, in case of irregularities in the walls.

**18** Then lift up the tiles, and apply a latex cork adhesive with a fine notched applicator.

**19** Aim to do only one quarter of the floor at a time, as defined by the lines. In fact, in large areas aim at completing one quarter a session or a day, as laying cork can be backbreaking work.

**20** Work a maximum of 1 m at a time. If you do more, you run the risk of the adhesive skinning, and not adhering properly to the tiles.

**21** Lay the first tile straight down without sliding it in place. Take great care in

## WHAT TO BUY

- [ ] 50 sq. m of cork tiles, including an allowance for waste
- [ ] 50 sq. m of hardboard underlay – say 40 sheets of 1200 mm x 900 mm
- [ ] 3 kg underlay nails or staples if power equipment is available
- [ ] 75 mm x 50 mm seasoned hardwood PAR, 3 of 2.4 m
- [ ] 20 cartridges of panel adhesive and gun
- [ ] 30 litres of latex adhesive
- [ ] 120 litres of polyurethane finish in gloss
- [ ] 1 litre of solvent for cleaning the finish
- [ ] sandpaper and float, or orbital sander

## SPECIAL TOOLS NEEDED

- [ ] adhesive applicators, 3 mm notched trowels
- [ ] paint brushes
- [ ] paint roller and extension
- [ ] vacuum cleaner
- [ ] chalkline
- [ ] power stapler (if desired)

## HIRE

- [ ] sander for smoothing floor

## TIME

Four full weekends

*The underlay is fixed across the floor and joints are staggered*

*Cork tiles bedded in adhesive*

*Marking tile to be cut*

*Coating the cork tiles with a roller*

aligning it properly. All tiles should be laid without sliding them in place.

**22** Lay the following tiles in the form of triangles towards the corner, butting each one against its neighbours.

**23** When you reach a wall, tiles will need to be cut. To mark the exact shape required, place a full tile over the last full tile laid in that row, and place another full tile over that. The top tile can then be slid against the wall or skirting. Use a pencil to mark a line on the lower tile, which corresponds to where the tile should be cut.

**24** Cut the tile with a straight edge and a sharp utility knife. If you end up with a rough edge, you may need to lightly sand the edge.

**25** Finish one quarter at a time, and clean excess adhesive off the floor as you go so that you will be able to continue from where you left off the following day.

**26** Clean all applicators ready for the next day's work.

**27** Repeat these steps for all other sections, until the floor is finished.

### KITCHEN

**28** Repeat the above steps in the adjoining kitchen in the same way. The steps will need all cut tiles, and the cork will need to be measured individually. Apply the tread tiles first, then the riser tiles.

**29** When the cork is down but before it is finished, it is important to avoid staining the floor with food, drinks or paint, or even stains from dirt or building debris carried underfoot. It is safest to keep traffic off the floor.

**30** Once the tiles are set (leave overnight), the floor will need to be sanded to remove any high spots, or to level where the thickness of tiles was not exactly the same. (Some variation in thickness is not uncommon.) You can have the floor professionally

sanded to level the joints, or do it yourself with an orbital sander or hand-float. It is a slow job – you must take care not to sand grooves or depressions into the floor. Use #120 grade paper. The dust generated is unbelievable and you should wear a mask with a fine particle filter for breathing.

**31** Vacuum floor again.

**32** You are now ready to coat the floor. For your breathing protection, obtain a cartridge rated for protection against hydrocarbon fumes, because the odour of many of the coatings is overpowering.

**33** Open windows and provide good ventilation through the room. Close doors to other areas of the house.

**34** Apply the first coat of polyurethane by brushing around the perimeter. Use a roller on an extension rod for the main body of the floor. The roller should have a medium nap.

**35** Once dry, sand smooth with #120 paper and vacuum once again.

**36** Apply the second coat of polyurethane as before. You start getting a shine with this coat.

**37** Give the floor a last final light sand and vacuum up the dust carefully.

**38** Close the windows to provide still, dustless air. Apply the final coat with brush and roller, and let this cure for at least 24 hours before light traffic, and three or four days before normal traffic is let on the floor.

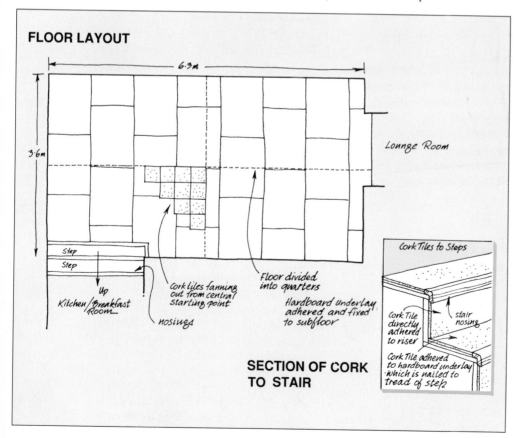

**FLOOR LAYOUT** — 6·3 m, 3·6 m, Lounge Room, Step, Step, Up, Kitchen/Breakfast Room, nosings, Cork tiles fanning out from central starting point, Floor divided into quarters, Hardboard underlay adhered and fixed to subfloor

**SECTION OF CORK TO STAIR** — Cork Tiles to Steps, Cork Tile directly adhered to riser, stair nosing, Cork Tile adhered to hardboard underlay which is nailed to tread of step

*Rugs can be a unique and complementary part of your total design scheme, adding colour, accent and life. In fact, a rug is often the decorating accessory which pulls a whole room together. It is a versatile design element, easily moved around, practical yet full of creative possibilities.*

# RAVISHING RUGS
## Traditional and contemporary

Your rug may be there to add atmosphere and comfort to a hard, cold floor surface, or to provide cheerful (and cheap) relief from unsightly patches of stained or worn-out carpet. A well-chosen rug will dress up a plain carpet, and protect it, especially in heavy traffic areas such as halls and corridors.

Rugs are available to suit every budget. They can be bought as part of a quick, on-the-cheap home improvement project, or as part of a more long-term financial investment. Although most rugs are imported, the industry is highly competitive and there's always room for a bargain.

### RUG TYPES
Aside from the traditional types of rug – there are basically two types: flat weave (where the surface looks similar to a piece of cloth) and tufted (where the surface is raised into a cut or looped pile) – there is a wide range of contemporary rugs available in all price brackets and designs. Those made by individual craft makers, rather than by carpet manufacturers, are a particularly exciting alternative, especially if you want something of lasting value for your wall or floor.

Rag, braided and hooked rugs are also part of a thriving cottage industry tradition, and will add a warm, cosy look and splash of colour and texture to your living room. Why not recycle your scraps of suede, string, silk, cotton and wool by making your own homemade version?

**DHURRIES:** Dhurries are flat-woven pure wool rugs available in a fantastic range of colours from pastel to bright, usually geometric designs, stripes and simple borders. They are extremely versatile, reasonably priced and very hard-wearing. Dhurries can be used either for formal lounge areas, or for the more relaxed, casual environment of the family room. They are at home on hard timber or tile floors, as well as on the more luxurious backdrop of wall-to-wall body carpet.

**CUSTOM-MADE HANDTUFTED PURE WOOL RUGS:** This style of rug comes in a wealth of different styles from very traditional through to ultra-modern – they can be made to custom size, shape, colour and design and are very versatile despite their formal, rich character. These high-quality rugs are hand-made from the finest blend of New Zealand and Scottish wool yarns – single strand, which gives the rug a tight, dense, velvet-like appearance. They can also be made in a loop pile, offering a more informal, dense look.

A rug which is uniquely yours can be specially designed to extend a room's decoration onto the floor as an integral part of your total design theme.

**KELIMS:** Kelims are wonderful old weaves (30 -40 years) from Southern Russia (Karabagh) and Yugoslavia – their most distinctive feature being very decorative and

stylised geometric designs, which make them suitable for interiors that are rich in colour, shapes and style. Kelims can look highly individual and different, and are handwoven in pure wool (woolweft on wool warp) to last.

**PORTUGUESE NEEDLEPOINT RUGS:** These luxurious, hand-made rugs come in many decorative styles – mainly floral for very refined decoration. They are hard-wearing, and will go well in any room. The coarser weave looks wonderful with a simple, more rustic decorative scheme which highlights textures; the fine weave suits a more delicate interior style. These rugs offer tremendous character and flair, and can successfully pull many design elements in a room together.

Robyn Cosgrove Rugs

### Picture Key
1 Blue and white striped Dhurry
2 Kelim from Yugoslavia
3 Dhurry
4 Custom-made handtufted rug
5 Portuguese needlepoint rug
6 Kelim from Yugoslavia

# TIPSTRIP

■ Good-quality rugs should be cushioned by underlay if going onto timber boards.

■ Secure light rugs, e.g. kelims, with mesh backing or nylon bonding strips to avoid rugs 'walking'.

■ Rugs benefit from being moved regularly, to even out wear and fading.

■ It's important to deal with spills and stains as they occur and not use strong detergent solutions, unless specially instructed by the manufacturer.

■ Beat the rug regularly with a flat-faced carpet beater. Vacuum on both sides of the rug, going with the pile, not against it.

*Clever storage is one way to give your domestic situation a sense of order – with good storage, you can go to any drawer or cupboard knowing exactly what is there. Just think, no more rummaging through drawers or piles of clothes on the floor!*

# STORAGE IDEAS
## Space – will there ever be enough of it?

When we have it, we tend to fill it. Good storage is making the best use of available space. If you like to be surrounded by all your favourite things, display will also be an important consideration in your storage plans.

Storage needs to be approached carefully and logically. And what's more, once your storage system is designed, built and implemented – stick with it. When you take something away from your storage system, make sure that you return it. Otherwise the system will start working against you!

Have regular and rigorous clean-ups. If you are a bower bird, your storage problems will naturally increase. Try to avoid clutter.

Now consider what your needs are. Divide your goods and chattels into those you use constantly, those you use occasionally, and those that are used infrequently.

❑ Items you use constantly include cooking equipment, crockery, cutlery and glassware, daily clothes and shoes, toys, cleaning materials, study materials, videos, tapes, records and CDs, linen, and the like.

❑ Materials that are used occasionally include tools, hobby equipment, and special clothes.

❑ Items infrequently used include seasonal items such as summer/winter clothes, blankets and eiderdowns, fans, portable

*Bedroom storage unit*

Lifestyle

heaters and Christmas decorations.

Some items may need special consideration, such as delicate materials and those that should not only be stored but also displayed. Often, glassware must be stored in a safe place where it cannot be accidentally disturbed. Silver should be kept in a dark place to prevent tarnishing. If you have items that you want to display, you will need the appropriate space and degree of light.

Decide which rooms individual items will be stored in. Who uses these things? Are they used in conjunction with any other activities or hobbies? Books should be easily accessible in book shelves but placed away from direct light. Records and tapes should be stored close to your hi-fi system for easy access, but away from heat and direct light.

Cooking equipment is normally stored in the kitchen, and cutlery and glassware in the family dining area. Clothes storage should be as close to where you sleep and dress as possible. But if your bedroom is very small, why not use a cupboard in a spare room, or a hallway, for the clothes you don't wear everyday? Evening clothes, sportswear and out-of-season clothes fit into this category.

Consider your items carefully with regard to security. If you have valuables it may be worth investing in a built-in wall or floor safe. If you live in a fire risk area, it is advisable to store irreplaceable items, such as personal papers, photos and negatives, and slides in one place, preferably in a portable container like a chest. In an emergency, these items can be quickly

*Storing wine in a narrow kitchen cupboard*

and easily removed from the house.

There will always be some items that are not needed in the house, for example tools, camping equipment, building materials, outdoor and sports equipment and luggage. Material being stored for recycling, such as papers, aluminium cans, plastic and glass bottles, is also in this category. Garages and storerooms are suitable, as long as they are dry.

Children and toddlers bring a whole new dimension to storage and display considerations. Height and reach have to be taken into account, as well as security of cupboard doors. Certainly storage of poisons and medicines need extra care, and a special medicine

*Storage unit for a small study area*

cabinet with a childproof lock is a wise investment.

In better storage shops and department stores alike, there are many storage ideas and systems available – some of these are excellent, others do not make the best possible use of space.

When assessing your storage needs, look at wasted corners in the house. Most household items fit best in square and rectangular storage systems. A popular storage idea for years has been to fit out around room projections such as fireplaces and columns. Circular and rotating systems will generally cause little extra space loss but, if using rotating storage carousels, items stored at the rear may be more easily accessible. You will not, however, be able to fit the same volume in a given space.

Finally, don't forget to utilise areas under beds, and over built-in and standing cupboards.

*This project involves building an adjustable shelving system for a family room, for storage of toys, games, craft materials and books. It is also designed to accommodate a computer.*

*Project 14*

# Shelving

## STEP BY STEP

*1*  Cut the shelving to length. The cutting list is as follows:

- ❏  2 of 3300 mm – 150 mm x 25 mm pine
- ❏  1 of 3300 mm – 200 mm x 25 mm pine
- ❏  1 of 3300 mm – 250 mm x 25 mm pine
- ❏  4 of 900 mm – 250 mm x 25 mm pine

*2*  Smooth edges and cuts with garnet paper on a cork block to remove splinters and any roughness.

*3*  Stain the pine to the colour required (if applicable). In this case, a light stain of 'Baltic Pine' was used and quickly rubbed off to simulate the aged appearance of Baltic pine.

*4*  Give the pine two coats of clear satin polyurethane to give a hard-wearing protective finish. Allow at least 8 hours between coats.

*5*  Lay out the lengths of shelving stripping on the floor. Compare them closely and make sure they are all the same way up. Ensure that the slots are all exactly in line when the tops of the strips are aligned. When correct, mark the top of each with a small piece of masking or coloured tape.

**The shelving is to cover the wall, which is approximately 3 m long, and can be up to 2550 mm in height. Space should be left at floor level to enable larger plastic bins and baskets to be pushed underneath. The best form of shelving for this purpose is an adjustable wall-mounted shelving system, and in this case it is to be fixed to a feature brick wall.**

*Completed adjustable shelving system*

**6** Measure and mark out the horizontal spacings of the strips on the wall, about 2400 mm from the floor. These will be at 750 mm centres to give adequate support to the shelving, which may at times have to carry heavy articles (bear in mind books are extremely heavy when massed together).

**7** Measure true vertical lines using a plumb bob through the marks on the wall.

**8** On the central line, mark the required height up the wall, and from there use a level to mark off on the other lines.

**9** Hold one length of upright to the wall at the top mark and pencil in the centre of the top hole to be drilled into the wall. Repeat this for each of the other lengths.

**10** Using the appropriate slow speed or hammer action and a masonry bit, drill into the brickwork to a depth of approximately 55 mm. Ensure that the hole is accurately placed on the mark. Repeat this for each of the uprights.

**11** Fully insert a plastic plug into each hole, and screw all the uprights onto the wall. Do not tighten completely; but let them just hang. They should coincide with the vertical lines you have marked on the wall.

**12** Move each upright slightly to pencil in on the line all the other screw holes, and drill, plug and insert screws to each upright in turn.

**13** At this stage, check along the wall that the face of the uprights is also truly vertical. If not, a small amount of packing may be necessary to ensure that the face of each one is also true. When satisfied all is true, tighten the screws firmly.

**14** Clip the brackets into place and make sure they are seated properly.

**15** Lay the shelving on the brackets in the required positions.

**16** If the layout is not quite as envisaged, the brackets and shelving can be moved to suit your new requirements. Clips which join the brackets to the timber shelf are also available.

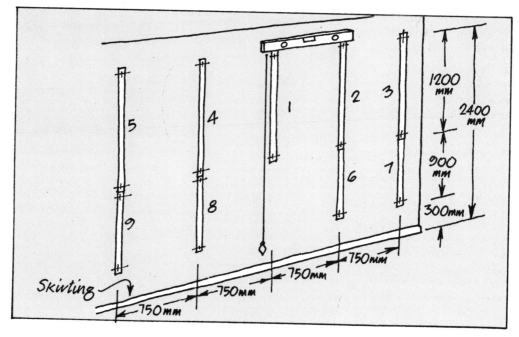

**SET OUT AND
SEQUENCE FOR FIXING
SHELVING STRIPPING**

*Books are heavy, and for the room which essentially acts as a library a more standard set of shelves may be the answer. The following is a simple easy-to-make design for an attractive piece of furniture made of pine. A cheaper version can be made of chipboard and painted.*

*Project 15*

# Simple Bookcase

**The bookcase consists of five shelves and a top, housed into two sides with a kick plate at the bottom to give it a finished appearance. The limited width of 900 mm will lessen the likelihood of shelves sagging due to the weight of books.**

## STEP BY STEP

*1* Cut the sides to 1800 mm exactly, and the shelves to 870 mm exactly.

*2* Lay the sides together; mark the position of the shelves equally along the sides and square them across the inside face.

*3* Insert a 12 mm straight bit into the router, and measure the distance between the outside edge of the router and the edge of the cutting bit. Measure this same distance from the lines marked on the boards. Clamp a straight length of timber to these two marks and they will act as a fence for the router.

*4* Set the depth of the router to 5 mm. Run the grooves along the fence, and move the fence for each side of each housing.

## TIPSTRIP

For a more professional-looking joint, stop the groove about 25 mm from the front edge of the sides to form a stopped housed joint. In this case, however, you must make a mirror pair of sides. To finish the stopped corners, a sharp 6 mm chisel used by hand will dress these corners square.

*5* On the outside face of the sides, mark the centre of each shelf with a light pencil line as a mark for nailing.

*6* Apply a line of PVA adhesive into the housing; insert the top shelf into the side and nail into position using 40 mm x 1.8 mm nails. Punch the nail head beneath the surface. Assemble all the other shelves in a similar way.

*7* Cut the bottom plinth to length, and nail into position about 5 mm back from the front edge.

*8* Check that the plywood sheet for the back is the correct size; trim if necessary and then nail to the back, also using a PVA adhesive and the 25 mm round head nails. Ensure that the whole is straight by comparing the edges of the ply to the sides and shelves of the bookcase. Sand the bookcase all over.

*9* Fill the nail holes with wood filler. This bookcase was then treated with a liming solution for a bleached look, and clear finished with polyurethane.

## WHAT TO BUY

- ☐ 200 mm x 25 mm pine or similar, 6 of 0.9 m
- ☐ 200 mm x 25 mm pine or similar, 2 of 1.8 m
- ☐ 75 mm x 25 mm pine, 1 of 0.9 m
- ☐ 1800 mm x 900 mm x 4 mm plywood
- ☐ PVA adhesive
- ☐ 40 mm x 1.8 mm oval nails
- ☐ 25 mm x 1.6 mm round head nails

## SPECIAL TOOLS NEEDED

- ☐ an electric router with a 12 mm straight bit makes the housings easier and quicker to cut
- ☐ tenon saw if cutting the housings by hand

**TIME**
Two days, allowing for painting

**TIME**
Two days, allowing for painting

*This project is a simple storage idea which can be adapted to whatever space is available. The design as shown will hold five dozen bottles. It is built using knock-down fittings and can be easily dismantled.*

*Project 16*

# Wine Rack

## STEP BY STEP

**1** Cut the steel reinforcing mesh to the dimension of 6 x 10 holes using bolt cutters. The bars are approximately 5.5 mm thick. The bottom edge can be a factory edge without projections. If the bolt cutters are held against the side of the adjacent bar, you will automatically achieve a 5 mm projection for fixing into the timber.

**2** Paint the mesh black. The job will take several hours by brush. If using a spraycan, it will be much quicker, but overspray may present a problem. Make sure you protect walls with drop sheets, or spray outside.

**3** Cut the sides to length, allowing for the wire mesh, the bottom shelf and ground clearance. Total length is 1100 mm. The bottom shelf should be 600 mm plus 5.5 mm, say 606 mm. The top will

*Entertainment at home is frequently accompanied by a glass of fine wine, and it is often necessary and desirable to store the odd bottle at home. Careful storage of wine allows you to buy good young wines when they are reasonably priced and to store them properly while they mature*

over-hang the sides slightly, and so is cut to 665 mm.

**4** On the two sides, mark in two lines 20 mm from the front and the back. Down that line from the top, mark 3 mm, 103 mm, 203 mm, 303 mm and so on to allow for the ten bays. On the top piece, the rows of holes are set back by 5 mm, therefore 25 mm from the front and 15 mm from the rear.

**5** Oversized 8 mm holes can now be drilled to take the steel. To protect against drilling too deeply, make a drill depth stop from a scrap of 25 mm x 25 mm timber so that you only penetrate the timber to 10 mm.

**6** Separate the knock-down fittings and fit the female part to the facing side of the joint, and the male part to the ends of the adjoining board. This will draw the parts together. The front blocks are fixed with the centre 50 mm from the front, and the rear ones 45 mm from the rear.

**7** Assemble the unit with the bottom shelf first; insert the mesh and then the top, being careful to align all components correctly. When finished, dismantle and clean up the timber with abrasive paper. Coat with a polyurethane or similar.

**8** When the unit is dry, you can assemble and stock it.

*Wire mesh being fitted to prepared holes*

*The 'great outdoors' has firmly established itself as an essential and important part of our homes and way of life. Home life is no longer confined to stuffy interiors and much of what used to be strictly 'indoors' is moving outside onto the terrace and into the garden.*

# OUTDOOR LIVING
## Making the best of your open spaces

Underfoot areas can be paved in any number of interesting and hard-wearing materials like pavers, of which there are many different types. Decks and barbecue areas blend with the home while providing an attractive extension for al fresco entertainment. Screens and garden dividers, and sophisticated garden lighting in landscaped surroundings are now common features of the modern home.

Paving, decks and barbecues are among the most popular home improvement projects.

Lifestyle

*Paving for an outdoor entertainment area is one of the more popular home improvement projects. The use of paving bricks is often referred to as unit paving. Pavers must be durable and non-slip – the most commonly used are made from either clay or concrete.*

*Project 17*

# Entertainment Area
## Brick paving and barbecue

## BRICK PAVING

*Clay pavers are very popular because of their durability and the depth of colour and texture that can be achieved. Clay pavers are fired at a very high temperature, this fuses the clay and shale together, giving it a very dense body.*

The other major type of paving brick are the cement or concrete pavers. These pavers have a large, more subdued colour range. Concrete and clay pavers are highly suitable for heavy-duty areas such as driveways and parking areas.

Both types are available in a range of sizes, shapes and thicknesses, to suit all applications, and to match new and existing outdoor areas.

The paving project here is a small area in the back garden, of roughly 10 sq. m. The site is flat and grassed at present, and the paving is to finish flush. Normal 230 mm x 115 mm clay pavers are to be used in a herringbone pattern. They are to be restrained by bricks on edge.

### STEP BY STEP

*1*   First decide which particular paver to use. As the area is just to be used as a patio, a 40-50 mm thick paver will be quite adequate.

*2*   Plan for drainage of the area and slight doming of the paving at this time so that rainwater can be quickly shed. Otherwise, your paving bricks will provide the ideal situation for moss and lichen growth.

*3*   Mark out the area, firstly with string lines, and then if you wish, with a line of hydrated lime.

*4*   The site should be excavated and all vegetation dug out. The depth of excavation is 50 mm for the bricks plus 30 mm for the sand. The ground must be well compacted to ensure that no subsidence occurs. Any soft spots should be excavated and backfilled with well-compacted road base (hardcore). If the earth is soft (as here) it may be worth excavating a little more, and adding 50 mm of road base (hardcore) over the whole area and compacting it. You should finish with a uniform surface with either a slight slope or a crown or doming

*A paved area with clay pavers laid in stretcher bond pattern*

### WHAT TO BUY
- ☐   10 sq. m of pavers (roughly 400 units)
- ☐   1/2 tonne road base (hardcore)
- ☐   0.3 cubic m of coarse washed river sand

### SPECIAL TOOLS NEEDED
- ☐   mechanical compactor
- ☐   long spirit level
- ☐   shovel
- ☐   rubber mallet

### TIME
One or two weekends

*Prepared base with tools, road base, sand and battens ready. Note edging already in*

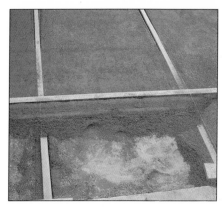

*Screeding sand over batten to prepare an even bed*

*Compacting pavers into sand and filling crevices with sand*

## TIPSTRIP

■ If surface drainage is a problem, an excellent edge restraint can be made of preformed spoon drains or 'U' drains. These are connected to the stormwater system, and will remove surface water flowing over the paving.

■ An alternative method commonly used is to compact the sand prior to the bricks being laid. After compaction is adequate, screed the area level, ready to take the pavers. It is easiest to work on a small area at a time.

■ A particular problem exists on sites where there is a steep slope. Here the tendency for the pavers to slide down the slope, may have to be counteracted by the addition of a small amount of cement to the sand bed. The proportion of sand to cement should be about eight to one (8:1) at the most, and the bed is prepared only slightly damp. The pavers are firmly placed into this bed, but when working with cement be especially careful not to get any of the cement onto the face of the pavers. When bedded, pure sand without any cement is once again swept across the area to fill up the crevices between the bricks.

effect to allow water to be shed. Water should drain away from the house. Do not allow any paving to cover either house damp proof courses or ventilation bricks.

**5** If drainage is needed it should be installed before the road base goes down. Subsurface drains set in coarse aggregate are effective in controlling poorly drained soils.

**6** A row of brick pavers on edge can be used to act as edge restraints. Commonly they are set in concrete in a small trench finishing at the level of the finished paving. In this way they can be used as 'formwork' for the rest of the job.

**7** The simplest method of laying paving bricks is to bed them in sand. Slightly damp washed coarse river sand should be used. The sand bed is normally 30 mm thick.

**8** The sand is screeded with a long piece of straight timber. Battens can be set into the sand to act as guides.

The level should be such that when a paver is bedded and compacted, it will bed approximately 5-6 mm into the sand.

**9** Start paving at the bottommost corner of the area, and work uphill. This small area can probably be done in two sections to make the job more manageable.

**10** The pavers are placed into position in the sand to the herringbone pattern and butted to within 3 mm of each other. Lay several pavers and bed them into the sand with a soft wooden board and rubber mallet, being mindful of the levels.

**11** Cutting of pavers can normally be done with a bolster and 2 kg hammer. The paver is marked gently all around, and then the bolster is used to crack the brick where it has been marked. Where a perfect cut is required, a brick saw can be hired from most hire outlets.

**12** When all the pavers have been laid, a small amount of

the sand is swept back and forth over the pavers, working the sand into the joints between the pavers.

**13** The sand can be left in place a few days, so that all the 'oohing and aahing' by visitors and neighbours over your handywork will actually help to work the sand into the joints. After a day or so, the excess can be swept off, and the paved area is ready for use.

*Casual, outdoor entertaining is an immensely popular and pleasant way to enjoy good food and good company. What better way to cook a meal for a crowd than a barbecue, in a beautifully paved, attractive outdoor area? This brick barbecue has a gas unit and a pine door*

# BARBECUE AREA

*Outdoor cooking facilities are a natural extension of an outdoor entertainment area. Most popular are barbecues, which come in an almost unlimited range of shapes, types and construction methods. They are normally wood or gas fired and may be as simple as a stack of bricks with a hotplate placed on top.*

The barbecue described here is a simple gas-fired one containing less than 200 bricks. It has a modest hotplate area, big enough for a reasonable party, and a small storage area for the gas bottle. The size can be adjusted to the size of the gas unit.

## STEP BY STEP

*1* To start off, provide a concrete slab on which to build the barbecue. The slab should be 100 mm thick, with external dimensions of 1670 mm x 600 mm. This size will minimise the amount of brick cutting necessary. This gives a total required volume of concrete of around 1.05 cubic m, which is just under four bags of premixed concrete. The concrete can be reinforced with a small piece of steel mesh to lessen the likelihood of surface cracking.

*2* Form up the concrete base with rigid timber boards. Level the formwork to the exact height and level that the finished concrete will be. That way, when it comes to pouring the concrete, the formwork can be relied on to give the levels. Old floor

boards 100 mm x 25 mm are excellent. Place the reinforcing steel on supports and pour the concrete into the form. It should cover the reinforcing steel by a good 25 mm, be well compacted, and screeded to the level of the formwork, and when the surface water has evaporated the concrete can be finished to a wood float or sponge finish. Let the concrete cure for about a week, by keeping the slab moist.

*3* The mortar for laying the bricks should be weak enough to allow for thermal expansion and contraction. A premixed mortar mix may be used. Weaken it with a little extra lime and sand.

*4* The first course should be laid out on the slab to check the spacing of the bricks. The standard mortar joint should be 10 mm. Laying the bricks out will also give an indication of where they need to be cut.

*5* Once correctly arranged, they can be bedded into the mortar. There will be slight variations in the size of bricks, which can be accommodated in the mortar joint. The spirit level should be used frequently to ensure that the bricklaying is level.

*6* It is wise to start at the exposed ends and corners of the brickwork, to ensure that perfectly plumb corners are achieved. The remaining bricks can be laid between the corners.

*7* Leave bricks protruding at the sixth course to support the gas unit. This can be done with three-quarter bricks, or steel bars can be incorporated in the mortar joint to carry the barbecue unit.

*8* On the top surface the quarry tiles can be fixed using a mortar, or a proprietary tile adhesive. Any mortar stains on the bricks should be removed as soon as possible with a straw brush, so that the mortar splashes don't set.

*9* If you decide that the brickwork needs to be acid cleaned to remove mortar stains, wait a day or two before tackling the job. The brickwork must then be thoroughly soaked with water, and then scrubbed with a solution of one part hydrochloric acid to 15 parts water (1:15), always adding the acid to the water. Wearing protective clothing, eye protection and gloves, scrub the brickwork with the acid solution until all the stains have disappeared. When finished, wash down the wall thoroughly with clean water.

*A timber deck in its simplest form is surprisingly easy to build. It is of a similar structure to the timber floor of a house. Essentially, a deck consists of a series of upright piers or posts which support bearers. These in turn support joists which run perpendicular to the bearers, to which the decking timbers are fixed.*

*Project 18*

# Timber Deck

## STEP BY STEP

*1* The size of the deck is governed by the walls of the house. The decking is to run perpendicular to the long axis. Normal bearer and joist spacings are 1800 mm and 450 mm respectively. Because of the size restrictions, our spans will be 1500 mm and 400 mm.

*2* If the deck is to lead out from a doorway, it is desirable to have the deck a step lower than the door entrance, so that in the event of a heavy downpour, water cannot enter the building.

*3* Working plans should be drawn up, preferably by a draftsperson, showing dimensions, directions of the timber components, and gradients.

*4* Set out the ground area. Footings are needed for the brick piers. Holes about 350 mm x 350 mm x 300 mm deep will have to be dug, for concrete footings. In this case, the bearers will be supported at 1500 mm centres.

*5* Mix and pour the concrete into the prepared holes. The top of the footing should be finished so that when the bricks are laid, they will give you an even bearing for the bearers. Let the concrete cure for several days.

*6* Three courses of bricks

**Decks can be freestanding, but most commonly they are attached to the side of a house for the purpose of extending the living area outdoors. This typical deck has hardwood framing and decking and is 2.4 m x 6 m in size. As the deck is low, it will not need railings or a balustrade to the back garden.**

can then be laid. The brickwork should be neat as it may be seen. Lay the bricks to the calculated underside of the bearers.

*7* Let the brickwork cure for a couple of days, then lay bitumen damp-proof felt on the piers.

*8* The timber for the frame of the deck should be a durable species hardwood or CCA-treated (chrome copper arsenic).

*9* As the deck is permanently attached to the house, no further bracing is needed. The bearers can be laid on the piers, and crippled if necessary. This simply involves placing the bearers on the piers, with the bow up, and sawing at a diagonal partway through the beam over the post, so that the thickness of the saw cut will allow settling of the beam onto the pier. Nail plates can be used to stiffen the cut beam.

*10* The joists are then fixed to the bearers either by skew-nailing (driving nails in from opposite sides at angles) or by using nail plates. Joists may also have to be crippled to

allow them to settle on the bearers. When the joists and bearers have been fixed, the base structure is finished.

*11* Decking timbers may be softwood boards up to 38 mm thick, pressure impregnated with preservative, or suitable hardwoods. The decking is laid with 4-6 mm gaps between the boards to allow

water to drain from the surface. Small pieces of hardboard are useful as a guide for the gaps between the decking timbers, but also check to ensure 'fanning' does not occur.

*12* When nailing near the ends of the decking timbers, the nail holes should be

---

### WHAT TO BUY
- ☐ 75 mm x 100 mm sawn hardwood, 5 of 2.4 m (bearers)
- ☐ 50 mm x 100 mm sawn hardwood, 7 of 6.0 m (joists)
- ☐ 100 mm x 25 mm pencil-round CCA-treated pine or durable hardwood decking, 58 of 2.4 m
- ☐ 2 kg 100 mm galvanised oval nails
- ☐ 10 kg 65 mm deformed decking nails
- ☐ eight 10 mm x 100 mm masonry bolts
- ☐ 2-3 bags premixed mortar
- ☐ 13 bags of concrete mix or 0.35 cubic m concrete
- ☐ approx 60-90 bricks
- ☐ bitumen damp-proof felt

### SPECIAL TOOLS NEEDED
- ☐ bricklaying and concreting tools
- ☐ hammer drill with 10 mm masonry bit and 10 mm flat bit
- ☐ string lines

### TIME
Three weekends

---

predrilled to about 80 per cent of the nail diameter to lessen the chances of the timber splitting. Normally two hot-dipped galvanised nails are driven in at each junction of a piece of decking and a joist. Stretching a string line along the row of nails will provide a handy guide to ensure that the nails form a straight, neat line.

*13* The deck could be finished with a decking paint or stain, but as a durable timber has been used, coating of the surface should not really be necessary. The timber will simply weather with time, and require no further maintenance.

Lifestyle

*Top: A timber deck in CCA-treated pine creates a delightful al fresco area*
*Bottom: Living room opening out onto a timber deck*

## TIPSTRIP

■ Supports for decks may be concrete columns, they can be conventional brick, or they may be posts of timber, concrete or steel. They may even be a combination of materials. Steel posts set into concrete are an easy form of construction. If stumps in the ground are selected, it is important that you use durable or treated timbers. A simple method for the first-time builder is to use a base of two or three courses of brick or a concrete footing, to which a timber post in a post base is fixed. This then acts as a column.

■ If bearers or joists are bowed along their length, they can be nailed straight by stretching a string line along their length. This in turn is used as a guide to pull the timber into line, before nailing in place.

**Whether you do it yourself or employ a professional, there are a few golden rules and tips to remember at the beginning of every home improvement project, besides keeping your sense of humour.**

*1* Murphy's Law states that if anything can go wrong it will.

*2* The axiom to Murphy's Law is that if nothing can go wrong, something still will.

*3* Know your limitations. There will always be some projects that a professional will do better and more cheaply than you can. If there is not enough time to do a particular job, don't do it.

*4* If you intend to build something yourself, check the building regulation requirements in your area. If you intend to carry out structural alterations you should inform the local District Surveyor's office.

*5* When building, remember that things tend to take much more time than anticipated. As a rough guestimate, owner-builders and do-it-yourselfers take three to four times longer to do a job than the professionals.

*6* When all else fails read the instructions (or get a bigger hammer!).

*7* Don't fall pregnant while undertaking major building work. If you fail this rule, make sure your size and the size of the job are inversely proportional.

*8* Children and major home-improvement projects are not always compatible. Sleeping babies will greatly limit the noise you can make (e.g. drilling, power sawing and hammering) so choose the time carefully.

*9* Remember – toddlers are disasters looking for somewhere to happen and

have a 12-foot reach.

*10* Kindergarten-age kids like to organise you to do their jobs: "Could you cut this? Can you hammer these together?" You will become expert at making wooden swords.

*11* Rule A: Do not lend tools. Rule B: If you decide to lend a tool, see Rule A.

*12* Try before you buy. If you can't decide what to buy when shopping for an expensive tool or piece of equipment, hire it first. This will help you decide the most suitable size for your needs and capabilities; or convince you that it wasn't really necessary in the first place.

*13* Three trips to the local hardware store will take about two hours out of your day. Make sure you have everything you need in stock and handy.

*14* When calculating the cost of a job, take into account the cost of hardware, nails and other sundries like petrol on those occasions when you discover everything you need you don't have!

*15* Don't assume that if you are doing something different (to normal) that it's wrong. You never know, you may have found a better way of doing the job.

*16* Keep your tools sharp. Accidents commonly occur when trying to force a blunt tool to do something it is designed to do, but can't in its neglected state.

*17* If you are pouring concrete, check and recheck all dimensions and the strength of any formwork. Concrete running out of

control down a slope, or setting in the wrong place, is very very hard to remove.

*18* Always shop around for materials. Normally the first price quoted is not 'it'. There is usually room for bargaining, so emotionally equip yourself to haggle.

*19* When using tradespeople or builders, ensure that they are qualified to carry out the work and belong to a reputable trade association. Otherwise, if something goes wrong, it may be difficult to have the work repaired or completed.

*20* When dealing with tradespeople or builders for any major work, make sure that you have a written agreement with the contractor. If in doubt about any agreement, have it checked by a building professional, such as an architect, who is experienced in administering similar contracts.

*21* Don't automatically accept the cheapest price quoted for a job. Get at least three quotes, and see how they compare. If one is way too low, be suspicious. As a general rule it's safest to go for the middle quote.

*22* Avoid parting with large amounts of money up front when dealing with contractors. If they are running their business efficiently, they will have enough capital to undertake your project.

*23* Don't accept shoddy work when employing tradespeople. On the other hand, be fair – you can't expect a 5-star job for a 2-star price.

*24* If you accidentally overhear a subcontractor whisper to a mate 'we've got out of worse ones than this before' – WORRY. Look and look until you find the problem – it could be something major.

*25* Most estimates of cost will be underestimates.

*26* If you are upgrading your bathroom, and it contains the only toilet in the house, make sure you warn your neighbours that suddenly and irrationally you may need to rush into their home at any time.

*27* When buying a house to renovate or improve, make sure that it is structurally sound and in good condition. If the property is in a bad state, more time, effort and preparation will be required before you see anything for your efforts.

*28* Plants with powerful root systems should not be planted near your home. The roots penetrate the pipe systems, and can dry out the underside of the house. You may end up with an imbalance in the bearing of the soil around the perimeter and directly under the house which can lead to cracking of finishes within the house.

*29* One of the greatest causes of building problems is lack of ventilation. Whether under the floor in timber homes, or through the house in slab-on-ground buildings, lack of ventilation can lead to a build-up of moisture and resultant mould and mildew problems. Throw everything open to get a good rush of air through the house whenever possible.

*30* Keep smiling. You are not the first do-it-yourselfer to make that particular mistake!

# GLOSSARY

**Architrave**: The trim around the windows and doors.

**Batten**: Thin timber member supporting sheets or coverings.

**Brick veneer**: Building method with a structural timber frame and a veneer of brick on the exterior.

**Came**: Sections of lead used between glass segments in leadlighting.

**CCA**: Chrome copper arsenic.

**Cornice**: Plain or ornamental moulding between ceiling and walls.

**Course**: A row (of bricks).

**Cripple**: To partly cut through timber to enable it to bed down properly.

**Expansion joint**: A joint of flexible material to allow expansion and contraction between two elements.

**Fence**: A guide along which timber or a tool is run to reproduce a certain cut or shape.

**Fish plate**: Lengths of sturdy timber used to reinforce a weakness in a structural timber member.

**Flashing**: A waterproofing material to prevent water entry at a joint of building.

**Grounds**: A frame applied to walls prior to panelling.

**Grout**: The (compressible) filler between tiles.

**Grozing pliers**: Special pliers for removing thin edges of glass.

**Hardboard**: A manufactured pulp board, used as an underlay for resilient tiling.

**Header**: The timber member over a small opening.

**Housing**: A shallow trench in timber to provide lateral restraint in a joint.

**Jack stud**: A short stud.

**Jamb**: The rebated frame into which a door closes.

**Joist**: A horizontal framing member to which are fixed floorings or ceilings.

**Lining**: Interior wall covering.

**Lintel**: A structural support member over large openings.

**Make good**: Return to original, or finish off.

**MDF board**: Medium-density fibreboard – a high-quality manufactured pulp board

**Mortar**: Cement, lime and sand mixture for adhering bricks and tiles.

**Nogging**: Short framing members joining the broad face of studs.

**Nosing**: Front edge of a step.

**Particleboard (chipboard)**: A manufactured wood sheet made of wood chips and adhesive.

**Pier**: Masonry column supporting structure above.

**PAR**: Planed all round. Timber that is smooth.

**Plate**: The topmost and bottommost members of a frame, to which studs are joined.

**Polyurethane**: A hard yet resilient coating commonly used for wear areas.

**Renovation**: Update from the original.

**Reveal**: Timber extension of a window frame to the interior.

**River sand**: Coarse rounded sand from rivers.

**Sash**: The frame around the glass of a window, normally moveable.

**Sawn timber**: Rough sawn. Timber is obtained straight from a saw mill.

**Screed**: Levelling of materials using a straight edge.

**Scribed joint**: A butt joint where one surface matches the profile of the adjoining one.

**Sealer**: A coating to provide a suitable surface for final coatings.

**Secret nailing**: Method of nail fixing panelling so that nails are not visible.

**Sill**: The bottom horizontal member of a window.

**Stopping compound**: A filler or putty for filling blemishes in timbers.

**Strip floor**: Strips of wood cramped together forming a floor.

**Stud**: The verticle member of a timber frame.

**Trenching**: See Housing.

**Underlay**: A preparatory surface prior to fixing floor covering.

---

## CONVERTING MEASUREMENTS

Although most people have some working knowledge of metrics, many cannot visualise what an actual size really means. Hopefully the following chart will help. The conversions are soft.

**LENGTHS**

1 mm approx $^3/_{64}$ inch

10 mm approx $^3/_8$ inch ( a mortar joint, thickness of the average little finger)

25 mm approx 1 inch (everyone knows what an inch is!)

230 mm approx 9 inches (1 brick)

820 mm approx 32 inches (an average door width)

2400 mm approx 8 feet (10 bonded bricks, or minimum ceiling height)

1 m approx 39 inches

1.8 m approx 6 feet (a tall male)

2.04 m - just under 7 feet (the height of the average door)

3 m approx 10 feet

**VOLUMES**

1 litre approx 1.8 pints (a carton of milk)

4.5 litres approx 1 gallon (a large paint tin)

**AREA**

1 sq m approx 1 sq yd

9.3 sq m approx 1 building square - 100 sq ft

## ACKNOWLEDGEMENTS

In the course of putting this series of projects together, many people helped. Apologies to any individuals or companies that are not specifically mentioned. Special thanks go to Jack Barrington and Pel Fesq (Gemini Studio), as well as Keith Atkins Bathrooms, Robyn Cosgrove Rugs, The Slate People, PGH Clay Products and Skydome Industries.

The Publisher also wishes to thank the following: NBL and Mitre 10 (Crows Nest) for supplying the tools for tool kit, pegboard and carryall; Ace Leadlight; Geoff Phillips (builder); Stegbar Door and Windows and Sydney Window Installation; Tempo Interiors; Creative Wardrobe Company, Advance Parquetry; Porters Original Lime Wash for supplying liming liquid.